TRUST THE CIRCLE

The Resistance and Resilience of Rubén Castilla Herrera

TRUST THE CIRCLE

The Resistance and Resilience of Rubén Castilla Herrera

PALOMA MARTINEZ-CRUZ

BELT PUBLISHING

First Belt Publishing Edition 2023
ISBN: 978-1-953368-60-7

Front cover portrait: Courtesy of photographer Katie Forbes.

Belt Publishing
13443 Detroit Avenue, Lakewood, OH 44107
www.beltpublishing.com

Book design by Jordan Koluch
Cover by David Wilson

FOR EMILIANO RICARDO VARGAS

Table of Contents

Acknowledgments

The time, labor, support, oral histories, and órales of many compadres, camaradas, and padrines de tinta y papel went into this book.

First, and most obviously, thank you to Rubén, mi gran maestro, carnal, and fearless inciter of compassion. From the first time I came to a Coalition of Immokalee Workers action in 2015, he urged me to get on the megaphone and speak. I was nervous, unprepared, and extremely cold. Grasping at an excuse, I said, "My fingers are too numb to work the button."

"That's okay," he said, breezing right past my reluctance. "Nick will work it for you." Sure enough, Nicholas Pasquarello gamely held the megaphone for me while I fumbled with the words that arrived at that moment.

I learned something important that day. I saw how "saying something" wasn't really about me. It was about the campaign and about respecting the space of struggle by offering support.

After that day, whenever I showed up to an action Rubén helped organize, I came to expect the moment when he'd turn to me with a cheerful smile and tell me to say something. Eventually, it stopped being contained to protests. It just became a general expectation, like when he and Nick came over to our house one winter for a tamalada. Our assorted guests were seated in the living room, busy over their plates. We were in a natural, circular arrangement with no particular ceremony or focus. When he finally spoke to me, it was as though he'd been trying his hardest to hold his words back, which made them sound even more urgent when they were released: "*Say* something!"

It was hilarious. He couldn't stand to be in a perfect circle with abundant food and company without pausing to hold up the moment as the unique and perfect gem that it was. Of course, I complied, and I was glad that I did. Not only was Rubén finally at ease after I spoke, but I could tell everyone there felt more seen and welcomed than they had before. There was grace in that.

As such, this book is brought to you by Rubén's refrain that continues to echo in my mind and that somehow has grown even louder after his departure: "Say something!"

This work is also the result of many wonderful people in Rubén's circles who provided their time and answered my questions. Nick sat with me on many occasions to go over the details of his life with Rubén. He weighed in on several chapters, and he was generous in pointing out potential inconsistencies or gaps. Also, the kindness and support of Edwin Woolever, which Nick appropriately celebrates in his afterword, was central to this book's flow, both in and out of the home the two share.

Rubén's older brother Roland gave me generous doses of Chicano humor while he eloquently described the Herrera clan's family life. My conversations with him were a high point of the pandemic's first cold and lonely year. Rubén's older sister Rosa María provided a crucial perspective on childhood in the Herrera family. I also want to hold up Rubén's older brother Ramón and his younger sister Ruth Marie here, too.

Hermanos adorados de Rubén: ¡Presentes!

Rubén's four children—Rita Herrera, Ruben Herrera Jr., Naomi Chamberlain, and Marisa Garverick Herrera—are all this book's favorite. When someone is tempted to canonize an elder who has transitioned to the next world, just talk to their adult children—they'll give it to you straight. There wasn't enough room to fit details from all their stories in the book, but every moment spent talking with them about their dad was a gift.

The voices of many luminous beings in Rubén's circle also made this book possible. Rev. Joel Miller, Nicholas Torres, Edith Espinal, Miriam Vargas, Thelma Sanchez Murphy, Deb Garverick, Steve Ryman, Rick Livingston, Laura Engle, Leticia Vazquez-Smith, Austin Kocher, Mike Smalz, Irv Hershenbaum, and many others shared their memories of Rubén with me or offered insights about the historical context of his activities. The labor of Elena Foulis, Latinx oral history superstar, was indispensable. Ditto for Josh Culbertson's *We Are Compatible* podcast.

One of my priorities in writing this book was ensuring that this would be a multivocal project that was as faithful as possible to Rubén's intention to celebrate all the people in his circle. Along with Nick, who contributed the afterword, Pranav Jani, Erin Upchurch, and Nick Torres wrote moving and elegant essays and/or reflections that truly brought Rubén's circle to life.

Fundamental support for my research and community engagement endeavors came from the Department of Spanish and Portuguese at the Ohio State University, the Latinx Studies Program, and the Ohio Hispanic Heritage project under the leadership of Terrell Morgan, who was key to getting this project off the starting blocks. The work of leaders such as Frederick Luis Aldama, Yolanda Zepeda, and John Grinstead remind me of the song "We Who Believe in Freedom Cannot Rest." I thank them for sustaining my time on the page.

To Belt Publishing for their vote of confidence in Rubén's story and their fierce catalog dedicated to social justice throughout the Midwest, GRACIAS. What an honor for Rubén's biography to have found a home with your press.

Encouragement came from an incredible pit crew that includes, but is not limited to, many friends and teachers: Dominica Rice-Cisneros,

Inés Valdez, Shanna Lorenz, Stephanie Smith and James Genova, Larry Bogad, Anthony Palmiscno, Leila Vieira, Hannah Grace Morrison, Ana Puga, Lisa Voigt, Pedro Pereira, Isis Barra Costa, the original Taco Reparations founders and engagers—Laura LROD Rodriguez, Bryan Ortiz, and Moriah Flagler—the Coalition of Immokalee Workers, the Colectivo Santuario, the Martínez family in Huautla de Jiménez, Roshi Randall Ryotan Eiger, and Katie Egart.

A special *gassho* goes to Roshi Enkyo Pat O'Hara, who gave me the dharma name "Enmei" in 1998. "En" means "circle," and "mei" means "light." The name and its myriad connotations compelled me to see Rubén's *ensō* tattoo (encircling the phrase "Hasta la victoria siempre") as further evidence that he was in tune with something that mattered to me.

The creative and spiritual support of my Pocha Nostra corps—Guillermo Gómez-Peña, Balitrónica Gómez, Saul García-López, Emma Tramposch, and Micha Espinosa—are central to the *Pocha* critical lens through which I view resistance, resilience, humor, and the stark, raving fearlessness that is particular to activists and performance artists. I love that Rubén loved Gómez-Peña, and it was an honor to have convened a space for their engagement on OSU's campus in 2015 and 2017.

Thank you to my mother, Rosa Martinez, who is a fierce convener of wisdom circles in her own right. To my brother, Camilo Cruz, for showing up to our lives in Ohio and being brilliant. To my late father, Richard V. Cruz, for storming Saint Basil's Cathedral. And to all my Cruz, Viveros, Osuna, and Mojica primas and camaradas—I love you all.

Gracias de corazón to Emiliano Vargas and Vanora Chapman, who now call Ohio home, much to my amazement and glee. Finally, my gratitude goes to Eric Hicks, who knows, as few others do, how hard the work of writing can get. These pages were brought to you by how many times he made food appear in our home. And joy.

Foreword: Trust the Circle

by Pranav Jani

It is incredibly humbling for me, and a great honor, to write the foreword for this book on my dear friend Rubén Castilla Herrera, whom I first met on May Day in 2006, as Latinx activists mobilized across the nation—and in Columbus—for a one-day strike and boycott. Thank you to my friend and colleague, Dr. Paloma Martinez-Cruz, and to Nick Pasquarello, my comrade and Rubén's partner, for inviting me in.

What a wonderful project this is, assembling so many voices and stories to remember Rubén, a gentle and yet forceful presence in so many of our lives that kept inspiring us and challenging us to expand our horizons. Written in a clear and accessible way, *Trust the Circle* preserves Rubén's story for all of us who knew him, and for the future so others can learn about him.

Trust the Circle is also a contribution to Latinx history, a "history from below" that enriches our understanding of Latinx presence in the US, and in Ohio specifically. In defiance of the flat, formulaic stereotype of Central Ohio and the Midwest as a "red space" (not the red of revolutionaries!),

Trust the Circle alerts us to the fact that at the heart of our social justice communities, there is a Latinx story, a queer story, an Indigenous story, an immigrant story, and a working-class story.

Rubén's story reveals that our community in Columbus is one infused with the lives and experiences of farmworkers, migrants, the displaced, and those—as it was written boldly on the T-shirt Rubén liked to wear—who will not comply.

Rubén's identity mattered to him a great deal, personally and politically. But it never limited his horizons of struggle and freedom. Rubén was a person who stood against oppression everywhere, regardless of whom it targeted, and he fought for liberation and self-determination along all lines—economic, social, legal, political, sexual. He understood that our liberation is intertwined. He left us with so much to reflect on and learn from.

I want to draw attention, right away, to the kind of unique project *Trust the Circle* is and the challenge of writing a biography of a grassroots activist.

What does it mean to preserve the life of someone who, while he was constantly at the center of so many movements and actions, never seemed to seek the spotlight but always uplifted others? How can you both focus on one figure and emphasize the "circle" of community?

These are questions for any biographer who orients herself around social justice work, around the people, and *Trust the Circle* takes up these issues seriously. How do you value what a specific individual meant to a community and not end up reproducing a "Great Man" idea of history?

You can preserve stories and narratives in a way that centers an individual so much that the rest of us become passive observers. You can memorialize in a way that creates a statue of one person that sits there on a pedestal, a towering hunk of cold marble looking down on us. You can construct a heroic ideal that, by definition, is so far off we can never attain it, one that we measure ourselves against but always fall short.

None of that would do justice to Rubén, who was a strong, beating heart of the struggle. Always standing in the moment, never aloof from it. Always standing with people, never above them. Paloma's work allows us to preserve Rubén's story in an active way, recognizing that when we preserve something in the past, we *construct* ourselves in the present.

We select and choose what to remember so we can shape our lives and operate with a clear sense of what we value, what we can discard, and what we need to improve.

We must look at leaders from many different angles because they are human, not abstractions. We keep Rubén with us by making his memory part of the things we do today, not freezing him in a past we cannot access.

We are marching *with* Rubén still. "*Hasta la victoria siempre*" is not just a slogan. "*Siempre*" is not just a figure of speech.

As I reread this, memories of Amber Evans—and Amber and Rubén together at so many events between 2010 and 2019—rush to my mind. For all their differences of age, generation, racial and ethnic background, gender, and more, Amber and Rubén will forever be tied together in our memories.

Naturally, the fact that Rubén attended Amber's memorial service on April 5, 2019, and passed away the very next day joins them together in our minds. Amber had been missing for months, and the sudden loss of these two people created deep wounds in our community.

Amber and Rubén are linked at another level though, too. They each played important roles, in their own unique ways, as bridges between different communities and movements across this city. From police brutality to immigrant rights, from fighting gentrification to taking on the Muslim ban at the 2017 Columbus airport occupation, Amber and Rubén always showed up to lead and organize struggles.

This didn't mean just picking up a bullhorn, going to the front, and giving a speech full of passion and conviction—though they did that well, too. But I mean leadership on the ground. They shared so much of themselves. They truly loved the communities they chose to speak for and speak with.

They were leaders who connected people. They turned dots into lines, then fused those lines into circles.

Amber Evans and Rubén Herrera, courtesy of photographer Ralph Orr.

What happens when you lose such people who hold us together?

It's been tough. The back-to-back losses of Amber and Rubén also opened up other wounds that have never healed, like the loss of Marshawn McCarrell in 2016 and the passing of Michael Vinson in 2020.

Beyond individual organizers, the regular loss of so many people in Columbus, particularly Black folx, to police murder and other forms of violence has created deep pain. We see the suffering of those facing deportation, of those confronting oppression, homelessness, and marginalization. All these individuals deserve to be cherished, remembered, and memorialized in all possible ways.

Some days, it feels impossible to recover from these losses.

We will recover, certainly, because the moment demands it. We will recover because we are a leaderful movement, and there are people who do this work of bridging and gluing together separate parts into a whole every single day.

But we miss our comrades.

I said we need to make our heroes human, didn't I? So let me tell you this: Rubén and I were always in discussion and always debating, sometimes pretty sharply. In fact, one of the things I miss most today is these exchanges. They did not *detract* from our connection but added to it. Because we could speak honestly and directly to each other, knowing that even as we did so, our arms were locked together as we marched toward a shared destination.

Free and open debate within activist communities is essential because the foes we are facing are deeply entrenched, and no one person has all the answers. We need active, dynamic, engaged exchanges of ideas even as we maintain the utmost respect and love for one another. It is a hard task made even more difficult at times by social media and chat networks that freeze our words and thoughts solidly, as if they were convictions, unbendable and unyielding.

As if we were lines that only met at angles, not parts of a circle.

Rubén and I debated about lots of things, but I think at the center of it—looking over thirteen years of work together—was the question of organization.

Some background is important. In all the time I knew Rubén (and for a decade before that), I was part of the International Socialist Organization (ISO) nationally and had actively been building a branch in Columbus since 2004. The ISO—which disbanded just around the time of Rubén's passing in spring 2019—subscribed to a Leninist leadership model, in which politically trained members (cadre) worked in coalition with many people and groups who were fighting for change, but they also recruited new members to their own group, which had clearly defined principles and goals.

As you can see, this model of organizing requires members to constantly proclaim their affiliations with their group. Whether it involved getting people to ISO meetings, getting them our political materials, or identifying ourselves as ISO members in speeches, the point was not *only* to build for the specific issue at hand (a police murder, a deportation case, an antiabortion bill) but also to connect people with a long-term struggle for socialism.

Whatever the strengths and weaknesses of this kind of organizing (and there's over a century of experimentation and debate on this in many different parts of the world), it was *not* the way Rubén organized at all.

Rubén's emphasis was less about organizations and more about people, less about printing out "where we stand" position papers (though he had *very* strong principles) and more about conversations, less about a public political meeting (though he loved attending our meetings when he could) and more about a gathering in which comrades cooked together and talked over a meal.

Are these methods compatible? I think so. But they are different ways of organizing.

Once, I said, "You know Rubén, one of the issues in Columbus is that we have so many small groups doing similar work, so many orgs that pop up and then disappear, it can lead to inconsistency and lack of sustained work." And he turned to me and said, "Really? I feel like that's our strength. Let groups pop up and dissolve back into the people."

These debates rehashed age-old—and important—questions about how organized activists connected with the great majority. These discussions were part of the fabric of our relationship. But because what we thought was not hidden but out in the open, our personal connection could remain warm and friendly. We never doubted that we were on the same side and had each other's back.

I think we recognized a commonality—that no matter how much of an "organization man" I was, I always tried to keep space for that human, organic connection, and no matter how much Rubén seemed to stand for "spontaneity," he was quite strategic in his thinking, someone who was interested in sustained collaboration and organizing.

As my own ideas about organizing evolve, I miss Rubén's critical, comradely feedback. Instead, I imagine his voice and his smile, and, taking a deep breath, I move forward.

The road is long and hard, and the loss of friends and comrades makes it that much more difficult. But by remembering them and reading about them, and by learning things we never knew, we make them come alive again, giving us more energy for our own journeys.

I'm so eager to see how people use *Trust the Circle* in their networks and their organizing, how we can deepen our understanding of Latinx histories as they intersect with various other identities and experiences, and how, reflecting on ourselves in the present, we can enrich our communities and keep rebuilding and reinforcing that circle.

Trust the circle!

Hasta la victoria siempre!

In love and solidarity,
Pranav Jani
Columbus, Ohio
October 2022

TRUST THE CIRCLE

The Resistance and Resilience of Rubén Castilla Herrera

Introduction

HAVE YOU MET RUBÉN?

> Everywhere you are is the center of the world. You're always standing in the middle of sacred space, standing in the middle of the circle. Everyone who walks up to you has entered that sacred space, and it's not accidental. Whatever comes into the space is there to teach you.
>
> —Rubén Castilla Herrera, May 17, 2010

The first time I met Rubén Castilla Herrera was on November 1, 2014, but that meeting was preceded by about a year of hearing the following question on repeat: "Have you met Rubén?"

I moved from Chicago, Illinois, to Columbus, Ohio, in 2013 to work as an assistant professor of Latinx cultural studies in the Department of Spanish and Portuguese at the Ohio State University. I was thrilled to move to Columbus and start my new job, but I was also sad to leave my Pilsen neighborhood in Chicago, a predominantly Mexican neighborhood that pulsed with Latinidad in every way: the Mexican street mural tradition, desayunos with handmade tortillas and salsa casera on every block, and, of course, the sense of humor. Born and raised in Los Angeles, California, Chicago had been my home for over seven years. When I moved to Columbus, I was setting up permanent residence in a place that was not predominantly Latinx, and in that first year, I was worried that none of these cultural treasures would be available in my new town.

Well-meaning people from the university community and beyond asked me this question about Rubén, but honestly, I wasn't very optimistic about the prospect of meeting someone in Ohio who really spoke my language. I mentally filed the question away, along with another repeated phrase I heard throughout my first year: "We have a salsa club." (While I casually enjoy salsa as much as the next person, my musical passions are reggae and punk.) These brief conversations with friendly, well-intentioned Ohioans just ended up making me feel even more lonely and adrift.

And then I met Rubén.

In 2014, Leticia Vazquez-Smith, artist and then-owner of Clintonville's Frida Katrina, invited me to conduct a calavera poetry workshop at her restaurant and Mexican crafts store. Calavera, or "sugar skull" poems, are a Mexican tradition associated with Day of the Dead, and they bring together the politics and slightly macabre humor that marks the aesthetics of the celebration. The famous Rubén everyone had been talking about was hosting a conversation he called "Circle of Life" at Frida Katrina right before my own workshop.

I was happy to finally shake this man's hand. His build was small but sturdy, and while his eyes were intensely kind, there was also a sparkle there of something feral and mischievous that I associated with the Chicanx sense of humor I so dearly missed.

There were maybe a dozen participants in the Circle of Life conversation that Herrera facilitated at the back of Vazquez-Smith's shop. We sat on folding chairs in the warmth of the shop on that cold November afternoon. In a gentle voice that was full of conviction, he told us that our circle marked a historical occasion. Our gathering represented a singular meeting of people that had never been in community before, but there we were, making history.

For our Día de los Muertos remembrance, Herrera asked us to say the name of one of our loved ones who had passed. What was something they taught us?

In my years in Chicago, and even further back, I had participated in Día de los Muertos practices, both in the intimacy of my home with a family altar and in the din of street processions that featured a riot of street-level ofrendas and costumed revelers of all ages. However, I realized that this was the first time I had sat down with strangers to say out loud the name of a family member I grieved.

"Kenneth Cruz," I heard myself tell the circle. My cousin Kenny had died tragically about three years earlier at the age of forty-three in a plane he was piloting. What was something he taught me?

"How to *want* to be a Cruz," I told the group.

I've always had a complicated relationship with the Cruz patriarchs, but Kenny was the kind of person who would show up early to help at a family function and be the last to leave after making sure all the chairs were put away. He'd been adopted by my Uncle Mark and his wife, my godmother Lynn. His birth mother, Velia, was the cousin of my paternal grandmother; her mental health issues had meant she was unable to take care of her children. Kenneth loved the family; he epitomized the virtue of coming together and he was—and is—dearly missed. For the first time in Columbus, in the safety of the circle Rubén had convened, I felt like there was room for my broken family and my broken heart.

The gathering he hosted that night, in his welcoming voice and with that anarchic glimmer in his eye, made me feel like Columbus might, in time, really feel like home. I also felt like my older cousin Kenny, always a protector, had come with me on my journey to the Midwest. Herrera had been the padrino of my first feelings of being aligned, whole, and embraced in Ohio.

And he still is.

The son of Pura Castilla Herrera and Alfredo Torres Herrera, Rubén Castilla Herrera was born on August 24, 1957, in Seguin, Texas. He died on April 6, 2019, at the age of sixty-one while gardening at the home he shared with his partner, Nicholas Pasquarello, in Columbus, Ohio. An Ohioan since 1987, he spent his early childhood in Texas before moving to Oregon after he and his seven siblings lost their mother to breast cancer when she was only thirty-six.

When Columbus lost Herrera in April of 2019, organizers, activists, and human rights workers across Columbus were left asking, "What do I do?" As a queer man of color with farmworker roots, Herrera served as a regional champion of intersectional identity and grassroots action. This book provides a synthesis of oral histories, community voices, and research into the areas of queer Latinidad and migrant worker activism inspired by his intimate and vulnerable way of seeing the world, as well as his role in it as an agent of change.

Herrera was not a hero-based leader but rather a convener of co-creative spaces. It's important to point out that there is nothing wrong with admiring prominent activists who gain a following for being courageous, personable, and effective. Their determination and hard work help to put a face on complex issues, and we connect with their experience while aspiring to emulate their skill in communicating hot-button issues in a way that will resonate across diverse communities. However, the hero-leader, and hero-based activism, has significant pitfalls, which tend to cast activists in one-dimensional, single-issue roles that deny these figures their right to human failings and philosophical evolution. A pyramidal organization means that there are many at the bottom and only one at the top, so the power is almost entirely concentrated in the near-beatification of the hero-leader who presides over everyone else.

Instead of a centripetal organizing style, in which the powers and abilities of individual community members are funneled toward the purpose of elevating a champion, Herrera's leadership was centrifugal, consistently redistributing leadership responsibilities and opportunities to the other people in the circles he convened. In fact, Herrera himself consistently pointed out to friends and loved ones the limits to his own appeal.

My interview with Laura Engle, Herrera's longtime friend, provides insight into his sometimes jocular, sometimes earnest propensity to be self-effacing. I asked Engle to share something "surprising" about Herrera's life, to which she replied:

> I don't know if anyone who knows him would find this surprising, but he was very playful and a bit of a jokester. He liked to laugh and poke fun and then mid-frolic, he could become very pensive and serious. My husband and he were roommates one summer at the University of Oregon for summer school (1985) and he said to my husband, "If you really knew me, you wouldn't like me." My husband could never understand what he was referring to, but I believe he was meaning that he had to fit himself to a mold so much of the time to succeed and be accepted and that wasn't really who he was.[1]

Here, Engle and her husband saw that Herrera hadn't wanted them to cling to an overly generous inventory of his virtues. Like Engle, I also suspect the remark referred to Rubén's rejection of the hero figure, where expectations about an individual's charisma and accomplishments can become constricting and burdensome.

Regardless of the impetus for Herrera's mysterious "you wouldn't like me" remark, it demonstrates his inclination to value the humble over the exalted, which is an idea he invigorated throughout his life as a public figure. His email and social media accounts were used to emphasize this theme. His email address was latinoleadershift@gmail.com, a micro-provocation that encouraged anyone writing to Columbus's "Latino leader" to think differently about what that "leader" title was supposed to mean. Likewise, his Instagram username was @trustthecircle, followed by a list of his interests: "Circles, color, silence, chaos, order, water, art, the earth, sky, fire, light, food and our cats. The sacredness of life." He sought beauty in the ordinary.

Herrera consistently drew on the circle as a way to elevate community, and he reveled in any and all teachings inspired by this shape. In 2013, the first year of his public Instagram account, images of circles dominated his feed as he shared a series of household objects. A plate and a strainer, along with sculptures, windows, bicycle gears, and coffee cups captured from high angles celebrated his encounters with this form. In one image, he holds up a chocolate donut and captions it, "Buckeye Donuts," followed by "#trustthecircle #circulove #columbusohio."

In another image from 2013, a photo shows his extended forearm emblazoned with his tattoo of a Zen ensō. The ensō ("circular form") consists of a spherical brushstroke to express movement, infinity, enlightenment, and, in its hand-brushed imperfection, the idea of (in) completion. Within Herrera's ensō, the words "Hasta la victoria siempre" are drawn, as if they were handwritten. These words come from the letter that Che Guevara wrote to Fidel Castro in 1965 before he went to the Congo to promote the revolution there. Guevara closed his missive with "Hasta la victoria siempre" ("Always until victory!"), which joined "Trust the Circle" to become one of the two signature phrases most closely associated with Herrera. "Hasta la victoria" appeared on his arm in cursive, with "siempre" emphasized in capitalized block letters. Instead of a caption, the Instagram post is accompanied by several hashtags: "#mytattoo #trustthecircle #circulove #hastalavictoriasiempre."

Herrera was so intimately associated with this symbol that the family and friends who created a memorial Facebook page for him titled it, "Trust the Circle—Remembering Rubén Castilla Herrera." A post on this site dated July 14, 2019, from J. J. Verbino is accompanied by a photo of the two men sharing a hug. Verbino's message conveys the way many felt about taking action with Herrera on the streets of Columbus: "The best part of any rally was always the hug from Rubén." Indeed, the hug was also the sacred shape of the circle, with Herrera's wide arms taking others in and lifting them up, redistributing love, strength, and courage to everyone who shared his vision of a kinder world.

Moving from his close circle of friendly arms to his public-facing sphere of influence, Herrera's areas of activities provide some insight into the causes for which he fought and the tireless ways he contributed to campaigns for social transformation. Herrera's youth in the fields of Oregon, California, and Washington gave him firsthand experience of the abuses suffered by migrant farm laborers, and his activism was always informed by the conditions experienced by workers that he witnessed throughout his childhood.

As an adult, Herrera began working on issues of immigrant rights as state director of Reform Immigration for America, a national organization fighting for comprehensive immigration reform. After Reform Immigration for America, Herrera went on to work in Arizona in 2010, organizing against Sheriff Joe Arpaio's deportation machine that included SB 1070, a law that would require state law-enforcement officers to determine an individual's immigration status during a "lawful stop, detention or arrest" whenever they felt a "reasonable suspicion" that the individual was an undocumented immigrant. In Georgia, he helped fight HB 87. Similar to SB 1070, the Georgia law included a requirement that businesses with more than ten employees use E-Verify to determine if prospective employees were eligible to work in the United States legally, and it made the intentional transportation of undocumented immigrants a crime punishable by a fine of up to $1,000 and a prison sentence of up to one year. Both of these laws amounted to the legislation of racial profiling, and they put entire communities in danger.

Many of the tools of resistance Herrera employed were straight from the Chicano movement playbook, and he was once arrested for performing civil disobedience fighting for immigrant rights in Georgia. Chicano social movements of the 1960s and 1970s routinely engaged civil disobedience to disrupt certain laws or regulations in a way that expressed political opposition beyond what a given jurisdiction legally permits. Publicly committing minor infractions, such as trespassing or obstruction, was an aspect of Herrera's nonviolent opposition on the path to seeking broader social change, and he consistently met violence with dialogue. Laura Engle recalled: "I remember a story in which he spoke of being literally under the boot of a policeman at a protest or rally and being able to maintain his composure, talk to the guy, and eventually wound up in mutual conversation, eye to eye, and speaking from the heart. He was always looking for genuine dialogue."[2] In Herrera's playbook, civil disobedience was not conducted as a theatre of anger but rather as a means to achieve dialogue. That was true even in the most compromising circumstances, even when his very safety was on the line.

While he had notably been at the forefront of regional campaigns for the rights of immigrants, refugees, and farmworkers, Herrera's activism had been wholly intersectional. A term that describes how multiple aspects of a person's social and political identities combine along a continuum of discrimination and privilege, "intersectionality" includes gender identity, class, race, religion, disability, language, and other ways that individuals and communities experience inclusion and exclusion in society. Herrera was intersectional before it was cool.

At the time of his passing, he had been organizing with the Columbus Sanctuary Collective–Colectivo Santuario de Columbus (CSC) and the Abolish ICE movement. He was a frequent respondent on ABC 6/FOX 28, a guest on *All Sides with Ann Fisher* from WOSU Public Media, and a nonstop panelist, invited speaker, commentator, and honoree in publications and at functions, including Columbus's annual ComFest summer community festival, the online publication of Appalachia Resist!, the *Columbus Free Press*, the National Association of Social Workers, and so many more.

His voice continually centered the lives of migrant workers and advocated for amnesty—a legal concept that would give undocumented migrants the ability to lawfully remain in the United States. His vision for immigration reform called for three core components: place undocumented immigrants on a path to legalization, protect workers' rights, and resolve the issue of family reunification. His efforts contributed to the Columbus City Council's resolution that supported Edith Espinal's and Miriam Vargas's rights to live as free women in the United States—a historical shift in the character of a city. However, even though Herrera won occasional gestures from lawmakers, his record of grassroots-level organizing, civil disobedience, and other forms of protest meant that he was more likely to be on the outside of the state capitol than seated at a conference table within.[3]

For over twenty years, Herrera was consistently at the forefront of many Columbus social action movements. In terms of the scope of his involvement, it would be difficult to find an area of advocacy in which Herrera did *not* participate. He spoke out for LGBTQ+ rights and the rights of refugees. He served as a founding member of several organizations including, but not limited to, the Hispanic Chamber of Commerce of Central Ohio, Educators in College Concerned with Moving Hispanics Forward, the Central Ohio Worker Center, and the Columbus Sanctuary Collective (Colectivo Santuario de Columbus). He was also active in campaigns such as Black Lives Matter, Ohio Fair Food, Latino Arts for Humanity, and the Columbus Taco Reparations Brigade. I hadn't been aware of his many firsts when I met Herrera and started to become acquainted with his seeming omnipresence in the social struggles I cared about.

My second encounter with Rubén occurred in the context of the Fair Food movement. I was teaching an introductory Latinx studies class and had invited representatives from the Coalition of Immokalee Workers (CIW) to talk about their work. At the time, I lived within a mile of the university and walked to campus to teach. That winter day in Ohio had been particularly bitter, and without thinking much of it, I pulled on my black cat hat—a knit beanie featuring two triangular cat ears that stood prominently on top. It wasn't something I would have worn to teach a graduate class or give a public lecture, but since it was an undergraduate class where I'd already established a solid rapport with students, I knew wearing a playful accessory on an icy day would not distract from my teaching.

During the classroom visit, the CIW team gave a compelling presentation to a rapt audience, and Herrera passed out fliers that detailed how to become involved and how to pressure the university to terminate its contract with Wendy's. Since 1993, the tomato crop workers in Florida had been working tirelessly to put a stop to human trafficking, to pass protections against gender-based violence in the fields, and to receive fair compensation for their labor. In that time, they have become the gold standard for human rights-based demands for humane and fair conditions for crop workers. As students and faculty at the Ohio State University, we had a unique responsibility, and unique leverage, to interrogate the university's contract with Wendy's, a company that refused to join the likes of Walmart, Yum Brands, and McDonald's in raising the living standards and curbing the abuse of agricultural workers. Considering the fact that, in 2021, the United States Department of Labor reported that 63 percent of the nation's crop workers were of Mexican and Central American origin, it is imperative for OSU students to understand how Latinx and Latin American migrants are integral to this country's food supply.

I was surprised when Herrera and his partner, Nick, came traipsing in as CIW collaborators and amplifiers that day. Having met them both only once before at the Día de los Muertos event, I hadn't been aware of their involvement with the CIW's campaign, and I couldn't help but feel that two new friends had suddenly appeared from out of nowhere at my workplace. Again, that feeling of home lifted my spirit and infused the bleak winter day with a warmth that only community can bring. When their presentation was finished and fliers for their next action—a demonstration outside of Wendy's headquarters in Dublin, a near suburb of Columbus—had been distributed, the CIW crew exited my classroom to enthusiastic applause and smiling faces. Herrera was the last to go. From the doorway, he turned back with a broad grin to deliver his last remark: "I like your hat."

As an activist biography that accounts for Herrera's personality and political priorities, the ensuing chapters endeavor to be both critical and centrifugal. As a critical work, this book fleshes out the complex social circumstances that Herrera inhabited as a queer Latinx in the Midwest with farmworker roots in Seguin, Texas. Taking a centrifugal approach, it strives to weave together the various voices, loved ones, and social circumstances that constituted Herrera's circle. By putting this book together, my hope is that his visibility will continue to incite spaces of gender self-acceptance, cultural and political empowerment, and radical inclusivity that his activist practices inspired.

As is warranted in a book dealing with the complexity of Mexican American identity in the United States, and given the range of words used to signify "of Latin American heritage in the United States," some notes are needed to understand how our diverse communities mark our identities.

First, there is no one, uniform way in which this highly diverse group refers to itself. Tracing the Herrera family's journey, they were US-born Tejanos who were simply, and problematically, called "Mexicans" in their hometown. Later, Herrera participated in the Chicano movement of the 1960s and 1970s, when Mexican Americans took inspiration from the "Black is Beautiful" message of African American civil rights struggles and reappropriated what had once been the disparaging term "Chicano," turning it into an unapologetic enunciation of Indigeneity and *mestizaje*.

Herrera certainly participated in the flexibility of cultural labels. He helped found the Hispanic Alliance of Ohio and, later on, Latino Arts for Humanity. His "Latino leader shift" attested to his comfort level with that particular label, and then he went on to proudly align himself with the designation "Latinx" in the last years of his life.

According to the Pew Research Center's 2019 survey, researchers concluded that only about one in four people who identify as Hispanic or Latino have heard of the term "Latinx," a term that coincides with a global movement to introduce gender-neutral nouns and pronouns into languages whose grammar is traditionally gendered along binary lines. First appearing in 2018, Herrera was quick to adapt it. Even so, it seems anachronistic to employ the term to his early years.[4] In order to use language that corresponded to the different phases of Herrera's career, this biography employs the term "Latino" to express the diverse groups of Latin American extraction residing in the United States when that was his chosen term. Evident in his latinoleadershift@gmail.com email address, he both activated the concept of Latinidad and called for its destabilization: a continually changing positionality, susceptible to permanent movement and redirection. As with Herrera, my use of "Latinidad" and "Latino/a/x/os/as/xs" becomes fluid when I describe events that took place later in his life. Toward the end of the book, and in order to address contemporary currents, along with Herrera's ready acceptance of its appeal, the Latinx designation appears.

I will trust the reader to be tolerant of these variations. They are the product of the need for group designations in the United States, and like "Asian American" and "Native American," they are also labels that are problematically superimposed on diverse ethnicities and nationalities but are adopted and adapted under certain circumstances as a "least worst" way to refer to groups who have important commonalities in order to gain visibility and foster dialogue around shared struggles.

The following chapters have required research into diverse historical circumstances and struggles for social justice, but they are all structured around oral history or recorded interviews (conducted by myself and others) to understand what happened in Herrera's life and why. While touching on Herrera's childhood in Texas and his early formation as an activist in Oregon, my writing places particular emphasis on the thirty-plus years he spent in Columbus, where Herrera's circle-based leadership offered a way to create rituals of centeredness that were helpful to the activist groups he led and advised.

The book's final section departs from the conventions of a straight biography. "Hasta la Victoria Siempre: A Trust the Circle Mix Tape" brings various texts and voices together. The "mixtape" includes a selection of Herrera's Facebook posts, my own interview with him from 2017, my "MenuFesto" poem that arose from our Taco Reparations Brigade energies, Herrera's organizing tips, introduced by Herrera's mentee, friend, and fellow organizer Nick Torres, and selected passages from a recording of the 2019 Broad Street memorial service, including the voices of Nicholas Pasquarello, Rita Herrera, Naomi Chamberlain, and Marisa Garverick Herrera. The section concludes with Erin Upchurch's reflection on Amber Evans and Herrera who, as expressed in several places throughout the book, will always be connected in the minds of area activists who were faced with saying goodbye to not one but two of its most important leaders in the spring of 2019.

Finally, Pasquarello's afterword shows that healing can happen in remarkable ways. And we don't necessarily have to move *on*. We can move *with*.

As stated by Pranav Jani in his moving foreword, when national media outlets and political campaigns take Ohio into account, the conversation tends to follow the formulaic assessment of the state—and the Midwest in general—as a conglomeration of politically conservative territories where progressive thought doesn't stand a chance. When the state revisits its unconstitutional congressional district boundaries, Republican-drawn maps repeatedly give advantage to their own party, and Ohio's status as a once-reliable swing state has been supplanted by its current reputation as a place where progressive voters are faced with the insurmountable challenge of their own dilution.

But this is not the whole story.

It's my hope that by heading into the material on Herrera's lived experiences and political battles, readers will know that they are not alone: they have a circle. Even while Ohio activists confront the most apocalyptic aspects of a postdemocratic reality, Herrera shows how one can respond in the moment to the most frightening social circumstances of our time and still find hope, community, refuge, and renewal in the small and large actions we take together.

Herrera's life shows us that resistance isn't just where we put our anger. It's also where we summon our joy, tenderness, and relentless faith in la victoria.

Chapter 1

WE MISSED A LOT OF OUR CHILDHOOD

Our planet's modern-day inhabitants have long been captivated by the Jurassic period, when dinosaurs reigned and the first birds leapt into flight some two hundred million years ago. Facsimiles of their bones can be seen in the exposition halls of just about any natural history museum worth its salt, and animated and live-action versions fuel adventure-movie ticket sales for generations of enthusiasts.

The less publicized Cretaceous followed the Jurassic. From the Latin term *creta*, or "chalk," the Cretaceous earned its name from the wide-ranging beds of calcium carbonate left by shells of marine invertebrates from the time when shallow seas covered much of the southern United States. The fertile, well-drained soils from Cretaceous chalk deposits resulted in a swath of rich, dark earth that arced through several southern states, including parts of Rubén Castilla Herrera's birthplace in the state of Texas.

Early Indigenous peoples of Texas include the Tonkawa, who lived in the southern Great Plains, and the Comanche and Apache, who migrated across the Cretaceous arc. While the origin of the Tonkawa's name is unknown to contemporary researchers, the Waco term meaning "they all stay together" is the accepted translation. A nomadic people composed of matrilineal clans, the Tonkawa were pushed south by the Apache, and due to their loyalty to the Confederacy during the Civil War, the tribe faced near-extermination at the hands of pro-Union forces in the Tonkawa Massacre of October 1862. By 1885, they had made their way to their final reservation in present-day Kay County, Oklahoma.[1]

Although not as screen-adapted as the preceding Jurassic period, the Cretaceous, whose soil led to the creation of America's Black Belt, continues to have its own kind of cultural mark on our times.[2]

Booker T. Washington explains the term "Black Belt" in his 1901 autobiography, *Up from Slavery:*

> So far as I can learn, the term was first used to designate a part of the country which was distinguished by the colour of the soil. The part of the country possessing this thick, dark, and naturally rich soil was, of course, the part of the South where the slaves were most profitable, and consequently they were taken there in the largest numbers.[3]

These soil conditions were especially favorable to cotton crops, and this led to the consolidation of power in the South in the hands of slave owners. Eventually used as a shorthand for political leanings, a history of profits born of massacre, violent displacement, and slavery, the Black Belt continues to echo in the material and social circumstances of the Indigenous, African American, and then Latin American and Latino migrant laborers, whose hands filled long sacks with cotton in the relentless heat of the Texan summer.

A little over thirty-six miles east of San Antonio, the town of Seguin, Texas, sits on the northern edge of the South Texas Plains. The government seat of Guadalupe County, the 2019 census provides a population estimate of close to thirty thousand, but Herrera's older brother Roland, one of the primary sources of information for this chapter, thought that it was closer to ten thousand when he and his siblings were born.

"Seguin was one of those little towns," he told me, "it didn't have anything special."[4]

Named after Juan Seguín, an early Tejano supporter of the Republic of Texas who fought against Mexican forces, the town is one of the earliest to be founded after the Texas Revolution had begun. It was also home to the infamous Captain John Coffee "Jack" Hays (1817–1883), who, along with his cohorts John S. Ford and Ben McCulloch, helped establish the Texas Rangers.

From before the Civil War until at least World War II, cotton was the cash crop of local farms. Guadalupe County had at least a dozen gins, and Seguin was home to three of them. However, agriculture was diversified with peanuts, corn, hogs, cattle, wheat, oats, sugarcane, and, most notably, pecans. Online recipes for Texas pecan pie will boast that it is bigger and richer than anywhere else: the real deal. Guadalupe County remains one of the state's leading producers of the nut, and a giant pecan—five feet long and two and a half feet wide—made from plaster over concrete has been displayed on the town's old courthouse grounds since Monroe J. Engbrock used his plastering skills in dentistry to make this tribute to Seguin's agriculture in 1962. The city motto remains "Home of the World's Largest Pecan," even though there is significant evidence that a bigger pecan now stands near the town of Brunswick, Missouri.[5]

Even with this small controversy, the pecan continues to be the calling card of Seguin's proud residents. However, it was the cotton crop that the Herrera children first picked, linking the remote legacy of the Cretaceous era's Black Belt to the nimble fingers of a generation of Herreras who inherited the struggles of poverty to which agricultural workers in this region have been consigned since the nation's inception.

Roland, like his younger brother, has held an impressive range of leadership positions. In Oregon, he has held a seat on the Keizer City Council, cofounded the Latino Action Committee, and helped to form the League of Oregon Cities' first People of Color Caucus. When asked to search his remote memory to tell me what picking cotton in his youth had been like, his thoughts went to the grief and poverty the family experienced after their mother's passing.

"We were poor once my mom died," he said. "We became migrants, and we were picking cotton. They would pick us up in a big truck. It was hot and horrible. . . . Oh my God, those long sacks."

Something caught my attention in the language Roland used to describe his family's experience. Across archived interviews with Herrera and my own conversations with Roland, the expression that the family "became migrants" was preponderant. While "immigrant" generally refers to someone who has left one country to make a final home in another, the experience the Herrera siblings described was that of *migrant* workers; they were people who moved for work without necessarily crossing a national border and not necessarily in a way that was unidirectional or permanent.

While Herrera and all of his siblings had been born in Texas and hadn't needed to move to another country to perform agricultural work, it was an economic shift, rather than a geographic one, that placed them in the circumstances of migrant workers.

"We went the other way," Roland explained.

We Became Migrants: Understanding Brown Labor in the Black Belt

When Rubén Herrera's mother, Pura Castilla, succumbed to breast cancer at thirty-six years of age, she left behind eight children: Raúl, Rudy, Rosemary, Ramón, Roland, Rick (who changed his name to Guido after living in Italy), Rubén, and, finally, Ruth Marie, who was only an infant when Pura's health declined. After her death, the Herrera family entered a new phase characterized by years of migrant labor as agricultural workers. The social context of this work is central to an understanding of

Herrera's political consciousness and the advocacy he performed in his later years.

Each year, there are about three million migrant and seasonal farmworkers employed in the United States. An estimated 65 percent of food provisioning labor is performed by people of Mexican and Central American descent, and growers and labor contractors estimate that 50 percent of the nation's crop hands are undocumented. One of the country's most economically, socially, and legally disadvantaged groups, most of these workers live below the federal poverty level, performing work in one of the nation's most dangerous industries.

In the United States, mainstream news sources, politicians, social media streams, and television, film, and other visual and print media make many angry pronouncements about whose bodies belong where. These stories, or myths, have a way of making it seem natural that dark bodies belong in the fields. This comes from the plantation myth, a genre of post-Civil War literature that celebrates the virtues of the glorious South and the tragedy of its loss. According to Matthew Martin, the plantation myth, which glorifies the institution of slavery, allows people around the country to ignore the issue of racial justice by making it disappear "beneath the smile of the happy darky."[6]

In the beneficent plantation fantasy, slavery is rationalized as having provided a sense of belonging, inclusion, and fulfillment to enslaved peoples, and they are often portrayed as being grateful to perform plantation work. According to this myth, this work should not be remunerated: it is already charitable for White plantation owners to provide their racial inferiors with food, clothing, housing, health care, and a Christian environment.

Enslaved peoples represent the early wish-fulfillment of the capitalist dream of work without workers. As modern agricultural firms moved into the twentieth century, advances in refrigeration and rail transportation resulted in a new distribution model known as "truck farming" that spread rapidly throughout the mid-Atlantic, and by the middle of the century, many of the legal structures of chattel slavery and convict leasing had been replaced by a new migrant labor regime that maintained historic notions of racial inferiority. Rather than being tied to a specific plantation, where workers would be employed year-round, this new workforce didn't pose the financial burden or moral responsibility that "ownership" of enslaved peoples implied.

Beginning with World War II, migrant farm laborers, largely of Mexican and Central American descent, filled the positions that, in the South, had heavily depended on enslaved labor. Although the Depression witnessed the mass deportations of more than eighty-nine thousand Mexicans, when the United States needed to prepare for war overseas, the US again went to the border to recruit workers.[7] The Bracero Program (1942–1964) supplied the United States with temporary contract laborers, while its companion project, Operation Wetback (1954), simultaneously detained and deported them, anticipating some of our immigration system's present-day contradictions, where a migrant agricultural workforce is simultaneously labeled as essential *and* illegal.[8]

While enslaved Blacks fit the bucolic plantation fantasy, in which unpaid labor was seen as a fitting exchange for being kept in a Christian setting, the undocumented workforce from Latin America was closer to the modernizing, neoliberal paradigm that grew out of the aftermath of the Thirteenth Amendment. The penal system served to keep Black denizens of the South in labor crews, doing work that enfranchised Whites had never wanted to do. Born of the logic that surrounded the convict leasing of African Americans, migrant workers in the agricultural industry came to fill a need that had always been consigned to racial "others." In this way, the realities of migrant suffering can be conveniently cataloged in the national imagination as an appropriate penalty, much like chain gangs, for people who have committed the crime of coming to the United States unlawfully.

And if they were born in the United States?

Returning to Herrera's early childhood in Seguin, if a relative amount of class privilege had been available to the household prior to Pura's illness and decline, her death precipitated an abrupt transition into the world of migrant labor in the Black Belt, where folksy songs about cotton bolls and boasts of real-deal pecan pie belie a sinister social arrangement that consigns Black, Brown, and Native folks to the status of pathogens and predators, and where the Tonkawa peoples, known by a name that means "to stay together," had been violently forced away.

Pura Castilla

> My mother died when I was four. . . . So that's a big part of my question in my life, and a big part of who I am. I think of my mother every day. And I think a part of my consciousness of justice issues is based upon that.
>
> —Rubén Castilla Herrera,
> in an interview with Elena Foulis[9]

Pura Castilla was born in Seguin in 1924 to Manuel Castilla and Sopopa Castilla, the only girl in a family of five brothers: Manuel Jr., Ephraim, Rodolfo, Rafael, and Jesse. A relatively prosperous family network, the Castillas owned businesses, properties, and a dance hall. The Manuel C. Castilla Park in Seguin, situated near the Bautista Emmanuel Mission Church, was named for Pura Castilla's eldest brother (not her father, who was also named Manuel). Manuel Castilla Jr. had earned a broad reputation of kindness, and he provided a community-level practice of microlending. Informal credit was extended to community members, but Castilla would reduce the debt over time rather than increase it, as would be the case with credit cards and bank loans. If someone owed Castilla twenty dollars, he would tell them to make it fifteen, and he gave liberally to Seguin's civic projects. Hard workers, with an enterprising and generous presence in Guadalupe County, the Castilla parents and five brothers doted on their sister, Pura. The brothers all went into military service, and along with their local standing as generous business owners who looked out for neighbors and friends, they became respected for their service to the country.

What had Pura been like?

In my conversation with Rosa María Herrera, she remembered her as a deeply loving woman who cared for her children with great patience: "She cared for us very tenderly, very lovingly. . . . I don't ever remember her yelling at us. She taught us how to love . . . to care for each other. Be there for each other."[10]

As the eldest daughter, Rosa María described her role as "sister-mother" to her baby brother Rubén, who was still too young to fully grasp the meaning of their mother's passing. On one occasion after Pura's death, Rosa María left young Rubén in the bathtub momentarily while she stepped into the nearby kitchen to do the cooking. When she returned to check on him, he told her, "I saw Mommy." He pointed toward the door leading to the bedrooms and told her he had seen her there.

"Well, she just came to check on you," Rosa María assured him, "and he was just happy with that."

Even though she was an affectionate older sister, she was aware that Herrera's life was marked by the loss of their mother by an unshakeable sense of loneliness, grief, and seeking that her own warmth toward him could not assuage.

Following Pura's death, the young siblings were sent to different homes. Rosa María, Ruth, and the young Rubén went to the home of their maternal grandmother, Sopopa, but this arrangement soon ended when their father retrieved them all to live together again under his roof. As her brother's primary caregiver, Rosa María had been the one most in tune with his emotional needs in those early years.

"He was a good boy. He was quiet," Rosa María recalled thoughtfully. Small for his age, playing and tooling around in jean shorts, his naturally sweet temperament belied a deep pain that surfaced in unusual ways, and he often suffered from severe nightmares that disrupted the family's rest.

> He'd be crying and he would hold his hands up, saying that there was something on his hands, and we said, "There's nothing there, mijo, look, there's nothing. Nothing, nothing." But he was crying, yelling, and all I did was just hold him and tell him, "Look, look, . . . there's nothing there." But several times he would wake up doing that. . . . They said that he was *asustado.*[11]

When describing Herrera's condition as "asustado" or having "susto" (fright), Rosa María explained that there were medical and spiritual beliefs and practices unique to "raza" (meaning her Tejano/Mexican culture).

Rubén Castilla Herrera and Ruth Marie, courtesy of Naomi Herrera.

Rooted in Mexican Indigenous beliefs pertaining to the alignment between the corporeal and spiritual aspects of the self, in the case of susto, an afflicted person suffers a type of shock that can cause the soul to leave the body. Symptoms of susto tend to correlate with Western indicators of anxiety or depression: difficulty sleeping, lethargy, nervousness, and diarrhea. The belief is that susto will not resolve itself but must be treated with the ritualistic sweeping of the body, prayers, and other interventions traditionally administered by curanderos (folk healers). In Herrera's case, his paternal grandmother, Julia, stepped in to provide the remedy.

"She did some kind of ritual on him," Rosa María explained. Their widowed grandmother, Julia Herrera, resided in a house directly behind the Castilla-Herrera family home, and they took Rubén to her for treatment. She performed a barrida (sweeping) for him with a small bundle of tender plants and leaves while he laid on the ground. "As far as I know, he was better after that," she recalled.[12]

Some years later, when all the Herrera siblings were working in the berry harvest in Oregon, she recalled an incident that hinted at the isolation that continued to haunt him in spite of the close ties she and her siblings shared.

> He was a good berry picker when he was little. Oh, man, he was a good berry picker, and he used to just go down the row and fill the crates real fast. . . . One of those times we were out there and he took one of the blackberries and wrote on the side (of the crate) "nobody loves me." I don't know why he did that. . . . I think I remember the boys being kind of mean to him.[13]

The family of eight was abruptly motherless, and Pura's absence was linked to an emotional loss that Rosa María understood could never be fully compensated by the care of a teenage sister or the curatives of a nearby grandmother.

Alfredo Herrera and Pura Castilla Herrera, courtesy of Roland Herrera.

When I asked Roland what his early impressions of his mother had been, he replied, "I remember her always ironing and watching *The Edge of Night*." The show had premiered in 1956 and was paired with *As the World Turns*. Airing on CBS, it was created as a daytime version of *Perry Mason*, which had been a popular novel and radio show and would debut on TV in 1957. The central protagonist was Mike Karr, who fought crime in the fictional city of Monticello (the skyline of Cincinnati served as the visual for Monticello's generic "Capital City" on the show from 1956 to 1980).[14] On their television set that was always in the vicinity of her ironing board, this long-running show about corrupt cops, vicious attorneys, and a broil of mobsters and their spectacular comeuppances was a steady soundscape in the heart of Pura's homelife in Seguin.

Another aspect of their mother that the Herrera siblings recalled was her Catholic faith and the depth of devotion held by the Castilla side of the family. Pura ensured that the children were baptized and that they attended catechism when they were old enough. For his part, Roland did not look back on this aspect of his childhood with any sentimentality.

"The nuns were mean to me," he said. "I don't know why. In my opinion, they were mean in those days."

As mentioned previously, the Herrera siblings were sent to live in different households after Pura's death, but this period only lasted a little under a year. Because Rudy and Raúl were older, they were able to stay in the homes of close friends, and Rosa María, Rubén, and baby Ruth went to live with Sopopa Castilla, their "Mama Grande de la Tienda." Rick ("Guido") went to live with Ephraim, an uncle on the Castilla side, in San Antonio. Ramón and Roland went to live with their uncle, Santiago "Chago" Zúniga, and his wife, Brígida, on the east side of town. As would be significant to Herrera's life story, Santiago and Brígida were Methodists who shared this faith with the young Ramón and Roland.

"I remember having a lot more fun at their church than in our Catholic church, and there were no nuns to be seen," said Roland with gusto. "To this day . . . when I see a uniform, that old school [nun's] uniform, I get shivers. I had a bad experience because I remember how they used to pull my ears and how they were hard on me."

Their brother Rudy would go on to become a Methodist minister, and Herrera later attended the Methodist Theological School in Ohio

(MTSO). "I always tell people I'm three-quarters Catholic," Roland said before adding, "I use it on my terms."

Because Pura had always been a stay-at-home mother, the Herrera's economic decline was not attributed to an abrupt loss of wages (she hadn't been earning), but there had been hospital bills associated with her care.

Another aspect of their family's economic decline had to do with the presence of their stepmother, Manuela "Nelly" Cortéz, shortly after Pura's passing. Following Pura's death, Alfredo decided to move the family to Oregon, which, as Roland eventually discovered, was related to the timing of Nelly's arrival in Alfredo's life before Pura had passed. "Later, I would find out many other factors involved in my father's life as a musician," Roland said, which seemed to be a tacit concession that their father's new relationship scandalously played a role in their material decline.

The members of the extended Castilla family rejected Alfredo, which also resulted in lost ties with Pura's children. One can easily imagine Pura's cadre of protective brothers, all proud military veterans and practicing Catholics, who saw the comparatively bohemian Alfredo and his new companion as a slight to their sister's memory that they could not readily overlook.

Roland could not recall if his father had accrued other debts besides the hospital bills associated with their mother's illness, but their family home had to be sold. If details were murky to the Herrera siblings, who were still too young to be privy to their father's activities, they knew that they paid not only a financial price but also a social one for her decline, which cost them the support network of the more affluent Castillas.

"He wasn't a perfect person," was the sentiment shared by both Herrera siblings I spoke with. However, when remembering their father, this acknowledgment was always accompanied by expressions of admiration for his enduring legacy of military service, musicianship, and community leadership, and real sympathy for his very human struggles as a father of eight at the time his wife became ill.

Alfredo Torres Herrera

> My dad used to say when you're eighteen, you either go to school or to the service. That's what they said back then, they didn't say the military. He said you go to school, to the service, or you go to work, and the key word is *go*.
>
> —Roland Herrera[15]

Alfredo Torres Herrera was born in Seguin in 1921. A prominent community leader from humble roots, he went on to become a decorated veteran while serving in the armed forces in Europe during World War II. "My dad was an insurance agent. He was a prominent musician. He was a radio broadcaster [and became] well known," noted Roland.[16]

On the paternal Herrera side, both their grandmother, Julia, and their grandfather, Crescencio, had been previously married. "And check this out," Roland said, "they both had exactly ten kids each. So you have ten kids and ten kids. When they got married, they had one child [together], my father."[17] Alfredo grew up as the youngest in a family of twenty half siblings, an arrangement that also led to one stepbrother on one side marrying a stepsister on the other. "They lived in ranchos far away and they were not related, but they became stepbrothers and sisters . . . and they got married. So my father had twenty siblings, and he was the only child of my grandmother and grandfather. I tell that story and people go, 'Woah.'"[18]

When speaking of his grandfather Crescencio, Roland emphasized community leadership, which I came to recognize as a family trait. In particular, the notion of social responsibility seemed to speak through several generations of their family. I asked if there had been any movements or issues that their paternal grandfather had been involved in, and the question made Roland realize he hadn't dedicated much time or focus to learning about his family's past.

"You know who really knows a lot about that? Rubén."

Fortunately, Herrera had used his Facebook timeline as something of a diary, sharing his thoughts on a range of topics that included travels, family visits, social actions, protests, visits with loved ones, and all the large and small moments in between. I turned to his Facebook page to see if I could learn something about Crescencio Herrera, and sure enough, the following post had been made on February 16, 2019:

> The Herrera family were part of a spiritual group called: Magnetical-Spiritual School of Universal Commune. It is based on the study of "eternal and continuous life" using its "Light and Truth Spiritism." . . . My grandfather . . . was a founding member of this spiritual group in Latin America with Augusto C. Sandino, a Nicaraguan revolutionary and leader of a rebellion between 1927 and 1933 against the U.S. military occupation of Nicaragua. Their mantra was: "Siempre más allá" or "Always one step beyond."

The Magnetical-Spiritual School of Universal Commune was founded by Joaquín Trincado Mateo, a Basque émigré to Argentina in the early 1900s. He had been inspired by the Mexican anarchism that philosophy professor Donald Hodges has characterized as "a surrogate religion, a promise of salvation through an austere, rational morality."[19]

Nourished by Spanish anarcho-syndicalist leaders, these early twentieth-century movements called for the liberation of an enlightened working class that were free from the yoke of ignorance and capitalist and religious forms of oppression. Arguing that the revolutionary Nicaraguan leader Augusto C. Sandino (1895–1934) had learned anti-imperialist politics and strategy from anarchist and communist groups while in Mexico, Hodges demonstrates that Sandino joined the Yucatán branch of the Magnetical-Spiritual School to signal his commitment to the school's motto: "The Whole World Communized."

Despite the location of its headquarters in Buenos Aires, the Magnetical-Spiritual School had more branches in Mexico than in any other country, and Mateo's admiration for the Mexican Revolution (1910–1917) was heralded as one of the important precursors to the school's mission of "communism without frontiers and private plots."[20] Hodges posits that, for Sandino, a major problem with the strict materialism associated with anarchism had been its failure to account for love and spirituality, which was how the idea of a "magnetic force" came to describe the sense of powerful interconnectivity that bound individuals into communities.[21]

According to Roland, the values of Crescencio Herrera had carried through to his son Alfredo. "I remember my father having conversations about . . . things that were not fair, and I later would learn that he had military friends that were Black from Guadalupe County that he thought were treated unjustly after serving the country." Their father had attended barber school to help his Black friends, who could not patronize the typical barbershops found in Seguin. Alfredo had also witnessed the mistreatment of his fellow soldiers in World War II. "He said that some of his friends were guards in World War II. They had to eat out in their jeeps. Even the German prisoners would eat with the Americans [indoors], but the Black soldiers had to eat outside. My dad would say back then, 'And you want them to salute the flag?'"[22]

The Herrera siblings, like their father, were aware of the social segregation associated with race and the in-betweenness of Mexican American experience in Seguin. When Roland was attending the Juan Seguin School, the student body and the teachers had all been of Mexican descent, but when he went to Jefferson Elementary, it was his first time attending school with White students. "Sometimes they would make remarks," he said, "and it was weird because we'd play softball and it was always the Mexicans against the Whites, you know? It was always that way. And we'd play dodgeball, and it was Mexicans against Whites, whatever we did."

In *The Borderlands of Race* (2015), Jennifer Nájera researches the policies and practices of racial segregation in La Feria, Texas, located about 285 miles south of Seguin. Nájera describes a culture of segregation that stretched into the late 1980s—well beyond the passage of major civil rights legislation—and was combated only by the persistent efforts and energies of the civil rights and Chicano movements of the 1960s and 1970s. Noting how the "ambiguous racial positionalities" of Tejanos allowed for some flexibility, the rules of racial dominance ensured that this mobility was contingent on how they engaged with the Anglo community.[23]

The Herrera neighborhood had been a mix of German Americans, Tejanos, and African Americans. Roland describes himself as one of the last generation of students to attend segregated schools, recalling how he played baseball every day with both Black and White neighborhood children, but each of them attended a separate school. At Jefferson Elementary, a school that enrolled both Tejanos and Whites, Black students had to continue going to their own separate school. "We were integrated before the Blacks, and then finally we were all together," he recalled.

During his youth, Roland was continually perplexed by the logic of race and national identity. He was referred to as "Mexican," even though he had been born in the United States, and when he was forced to fill out paperwork that limited racial identity to Black or White, the advice he received was to check the box for White.

It's a difficult image to take in: the untethered joy of neighborhood children bounding out of the house to play together on a street where they all slept and ate and fielded fly balls, only to be sorted by a school system that forcibly interrupted their natural flow of camaraderie and mutual respect.

Seguin Was Known for Its Músicos

If Roland depicted Seguin as a sleepy town where nothing happened, he made one important exception: "One thing Seguin was known for is the músicos. There's great músicos."[24]

Out of nearby San Antonio, any lowrider or Chicano oldies compilation worth its salt will include Sunny and the Sunliner's recording of "Smile Now, Cry Later." And their hit recording "Talk to Me" was released on Tear Drop Records in 1963, earning them a number four position on the adult contemporary chart, the twelfth spot on the US Billboard R and B chart, and an invitation to perform on Dick Clark's *American Bandstand*—the first Tejano band to be featured there.[25] Roland knew Sunny Ozuna, the band's leader, personally. "He always told me that they would always go to Seguin to get the músicos," he told me, "their sax players or their guitar players."[26]

The children's older brother Rudy had been a member of the Broken Hearts, a band formed in 1959 that was inducted into both the National Hispanic Music Hall of Fame and the Tejano Roots Hall of Fame.

The Broken Hearts started in the Barrio de Newton Avenue in Seguin. I was easily able to find videos of "Peligro," "El corrido de Sixto Sánchez," "Me piden," and other Broken Hearts recordings online. A Facebook post from September 2017 announced a weekend performance of the Broken Hearts, celebrating the band's popularity in the fifties and sixties and its influence on the eclectic sound that pulled from many sources to create Tejano hits. Ramón Salazar, one of the band's founders, remarked, "We never ran out of guys in talent. We ran out of singers, but we didn't run out of musicians. There was plenty of musicians and there still are. There are a lot of musicians here in Seguin."[27]

Tejano music, which emerged from the cultural border between Northern Mexico and the Southwest United States, is characterized by the blending of distinct cultural influences. In the 1960s and 1970s, the sound was characterized by the brassy orquestas popularized by groups such as Little Joe, the Latin Breed, and the aforementioned Sunny Ozuna.[28]

Epitomizing Seguin's reputation as a musical mecca, Alfredo Herrera began playing violin when he was seven, and later on, he played the saxophone, piano, and clarinet. "He played anything, you name it," said Roland. While the soundtrack inside the Castilla-Herrera home may have been dominated by *The Edge of Night*, Alfredo's nocturnal audial world was made of the unique confluence of the accordion-polka "oom-pah-pah" that German immigrants brought to Northern Mexico in the 1830s, rural conjunto Mexican folk music, and the urban, swing band sounds popular in the 1930s and 1940s.[29]

Unlike orquestas, conjunto groups are associated with ranchero (country) rural experience and are dominated by the accordion and the bajo sexto (the twelve-string bass). Conjuntos had been more widespread during Alfredo's childhood. Ethnomusicologist Manuel Peña notes that under the patronage of a small middle class, the Tejano orquestas were especially active in urban areas such as San Antonio, which was where Alfredo made his mark.[30]

Alfredo continually played in orquestas, and he eventually brought Rudy into the band as a drummer. This part would later be filled by Roland, and later by Herrera. Roland recalled being in nightclubs with their father at the age of ten:

> We played a nightclub in San Antonio called El Íntimo. And I remember because this was about 1964. . . . They'd have to chaperone me out during the breaks, and it opened my eyes to a lot of things. I'd see couples making out and I played with my little toys and come back to play music and in intermission go out. That's how we got our gigs, that was where we made our money.[31]

They All Stay Together

> To be with her is an honor and I feel I connected with my mother who I lost when I was four years young. I love to listen to her stories of their friendship and of their younger years. I asked her what was her secret to staying healthy and wise for so long and she answered with no hesitation: "It's my Indian blood." What a joy. We must always honor our elders.
>
> —Rubén Herrera, Facebook Post[32]

In 2018, Herrera and Pasquarello went to Texas and visited with Herrera's aunt Alice Castilla at her home in San Antonio. "She is the last living elder on the Castilla side of my family," Herrera says in his Facebook post. She was his tía by marriage to his tío Ralph, one of his mother's brothers. The lifelong pursuit to be close to his mother and know her better is tempered in the post by the wisdom of a man who, by then, had reached midlife and come to see his mother's wider community and the ranging Texas turf with gratitude and appreciation rather than through the confining lens of grief.

Of his younger brother's visit to Texas in 2018, Roland said, "The last visit was really weird because it was almost like he knew it was the last time in Texas." When I spoke with Pasquarello about their visit, he agreed that the experience had the feeling of a "final lap." They visited cemeteries in Seguin, and Herrera was able to physically reconcile with his maternal and ancestral roots before moving on. "He strongly identified as Texan. He lived in Seguin until he was seven, but that's definitely his homeland," Pasquarello affirmed.[33]

Shortly after the appearance of their new stepmother, Nelly, the Herrera siblings were reunited into the same household again. At first, Roland had not understood the air of scandal that accompanied his father's situation. "You know, you hear things later," he said, referring to his visits to Seguin in the early seventies. His musician friends and his father's contemporaries would make comments along the lines of, "Whoa, now your dad was quite a guy," alluding to his musician's lifestyle of heavy vice and extramarital entanglements. When Roland heard these comments, he was forced to reflect on how he and his other siblings had also begun to pick up on some of those cavalier behaviors, and it also made him more aware of the meaning behind Nelly's appearance in the family.

"I knew that my mother was not well for a long time," he said. "And I know that he developed a relationship with a nurse from Lockhart, Texas, by the name of Nelly Cortéz, who, by the way, she was really nice with us." He qualified his appreciation of Nelly by noting, "She *did* come into a family of eight kids." Roland didn't think an entire year went by after Pura's death before Nelly became a member of the household, and there were varying levels of resentment among the siblings for some of their father's tendencies as a womanizer, problem drinker, and strict parent who easily doled out physical punishment.

> When Rubén and I talked, Rubén had . . . a little bit of resentment about my dad at one time. And we talked about it because . . . I choose to remember the dad that, you know, not the one that was drunk and doing stupid things and hitting people and hitting us . . . it'd be child abuse now. But we finally came to terms with . . . his good points.[34]

Roland acknowledged that he was in a better position to hold a favorable opinion about his stepmother than his sister Rosa María. He benefitted from having the opportunity to get to know Nelly, who went on to share a stage with the Herreras as a bandmate and fellow artist, while Rosa María was consigned to the role of a young housekeeper, burdened with raising her siblings and keeping the house in order. She was seldom allowed out of the house to attend their shows, and she had to answer to a new disciplinary regime that would forever haunt her.

In spite of the complicated timing, Roland credited Nelly with providing Alfredo with some of the strength and resolve needed to bring all of his children together again.

"We all have our flaws," Roland observed, "but I remember she came at the right time in my life. It sure helped."[35]

After a year of residing in different households, the siblings moved in with Alfredo and Nelly, cobbling a precarious living together across many different jobs and living in a series of small homes before landing in the Casa Grande, a single-family home that they nicknamed "the haunted house." The house sat on part of the property that had belonged to the

Herrera grandparents and where their paternal grandmother, Julia (who had administered Herrera's barrida), continued to live in a separate house in the back.

Some five years after Pura's death, the Herreras and Nelly all struck out for Oregon. They left behind the Cretaceous era's Black Belt of pecans and cotton, as well as a clan of Castilla brothers and extended relations who had little tolerance for one of Seguin's prized músicos.

By all available accounts, they were not disappointed to see him go.

Chapter II

THE MUSIC AND THE MOVEMENT

The Herrera Family in Oregon

> I used to pick broccoli when I was a kid, it was the worst job. Because it grew as a big plant and you had to have this knife that sometimes you would get cut with. . . . It has lots of leaves in it, a healthy broccoli plant, and those leaves hold water. . . . You know sometimes how you have your hands wrinkle? That's the way your body would be at the end of the day, . . . so I get reminded a lot, especially those products that I picked. . . . Anytime I go grocery shopping or eat, I always ask myself, I wonder who picked this?
>
> —Rubén Castilla Herrera[1]

Before the soaring song and grunted snorts of the Jurassic's first birds and mammals, its preceding Triassic period, some 250 million years before our current era, witnessed the rise of reptiles and debuted the planet's first-ever dinosaurs. Oregon's lush soils that we know today were being composed at that time, when the Willamette basin was covered by the Triassic's vast oceans, where much of life's history on our planet took place. Sedimentary rock, such as the sandstone, siltstone, and mudstone of Western Oregon, recount the Triassic's story in its expanse of light-colored, well-drained topsoil—the mineral memory of this bygone world beneath the waves. Perfect for planting, the topsoil's low fertility is actually a boon to the berry farmer: it compels plants to send their roots deep in search of nutrients and water, making Oregon's coast particularly conducive to the cultivation of blueberries, strawberries, blackberries, raspberries, kiwifruit, table grapes, wine grapes, gooseberries, currants, and more.[2]

In the mid-nineteenth century, the Willamette Valley was home to over twenty tribes and bands of Kalapuya, Molala, and Chinook peoples. These Indigenous people lived in defined domains, where their ancestors had hunted, gathered, fished, and traded for over fourteen thousand years.[3] The European-descended migrants who ventured west encountered rich soils ideal for agriculture, sending reports eastward about this "Edenic" environment and evoking a "return to paradise" mythology that would compel tens of thousands in the East and Midwest to travel west on the Oregon Trail in the 1840s.[4]

On St. Valentine's Day in 1859, Oregon was admitted to the Union as the thirty-third state, closely following Texas (1845) in order to maintain a balance between free states and slave states. However, this did not mean that Oregon's history was untarnished by the violence of White supremacy. In 1848, the territorial government made it illegal for any "Negro or Mulatto" to live in Oregon Country. In 1857, the exclusion of Blacks was codified by the state's constitution: "No free negro or mulatto, not residing in this State at the time of the adoption of this constitution, shall ever come, reside, or be within this State, or hold any real estate, or make any contract, or maintain any suit therein."[5]

After the arrival of the Oregon Central Railroad (West Side Company), the city of Woodburn was platted in 1871 and incorporated in 1889.[6] Located in Marion County, Woodburn is in the northern end of the Willamette Valley between Portland and Salem. It is also where Rubén Herrera's family moved when he was seven. Oregon would be his home until he became an Ohioan in 1987. Like Texas, the Beaver State is another site where the geological clock created a set of circumstances where the human drama of race, class, and gender would take place against the backdrop of the soil's vitality.

You Have to Get Educated So You Can Work in Air Conditioning

When Alfredo and Nelly arrived in Woodburn with the eight Herrera children, they briefly lived with Pilar Medina, Alfredo's friend from childhood, before moving to a labor camp. Some growers run labor camps on their property to house migrant populations of seasonal workers who travel with their families around the Pacific Northwest.

"That's where a lot of us picked up our Russian, we lived with Russian folk," Roland recounted. Alfredo came to speak conversational Russian, and Roland acquired an even higher degree of proficiency since he had a Russian girlfriend. The young Herrera did not have the chance to become fluent, but he learned a respectable number of phrases.[7]

As the Herrera family's polyglossia suggests, Woodburn is home to a significant number of Russian expats and their descendants, including a sizeable community of Russian Orthodox Old Believers, a group of Eastern Orthodox Christians that maintains liturgical and ritual fealty to the Russian Orthodox Church with practices that predate reforms implemented in the seventeenth century.[8]

Within the context of these Old Believers and other Russian communities who called Woodburn home, the Bracero Program of World War II resulted in the presence of over fifteen thousand Mexican-born laborers in Oregon between 1942 and 1947 and represented a significant increase in the Latin American population. As described in chapter 1, Operation Wetback followed in the wake of the Bracero Program to round up undocumented Mexicans for deportation, even though many of Oregon's growers outwardly preferred and recruited these undocumented workers.

During the 1940s, both nonauthorized migration and contracted labor migration ran parallel to one another. By the 1950s, Tejano farm laborers (born in the United States) faced fewer opportunities to work in the fields in their native state. Job scarcity was fueled by land consolidation, increased migration from Mexico, mechanization, and new irrigation techniques. Oregon was to become home to significant numbers of Tejanos who arrived to perform seasonal work, and over time, they would put down new roots. Joined by Mexican American workers from other states in the Southwest and former braceros who remained in the US after their contracts expired, Oregon in the 1950s was host to an unofficial continuation of the Bracero Program that, instead of ending, simply went underground.[9]

Across extant interviews with Herrera, and through my conversations with his family members, all agreed that Herrera showed a remarkable talent as a fruit picker—a discovery they made when he was still a small child. Recalling the move from Texas to Oregon, Roland recalls Herrera's speed in the fields: "He was amazing. He would out pick anybody. I mean, he was picking like an adult." When their father discovered that he was an exceptional picker, "Man, that stock went way up."[10]

Rosa María also remembered his unique ability. As quoted in the previous chapter, her recollection contained an air of awe: "Oh, man, he was good picker. He would just go all the way down the row and fill crates real fast."[11] Herrera himself acknowledged across various interviews that his skill earned him distinction and privilege in the family: "I was gifted in that I was a good producer, I was a fast laborer. And so, in our family that meant more income, right? Because we were child laborers. So my value in my family went up. . . . I think I was even fed better than my siblings who weren't as fast."[12]

The Herreras were familiar with the difficulties of poverty and hunger—never to a point of being malnourished but also no strangers to tightening the belt. Before their meals, the family offered a simple, twelve-word devotion: "Come, Lord Jesus, be our guest, may our daily food be blessed." Herrera would forever be impressed by how this moment of gratitude centered the whole family on food, community, and blessing, and he would go on to share this tradition with his own children when he became a father himself.

Life in Oregon not only meant hard work in the fields under the yoke of poverty, but it was also a time of adjusting to a new family dynamic. Remembering their stepmother, Nelly, as having a pronounced Texas twang in her voice and a disinclination toward household chores, Rosa María found herself assuming the role of housekeeper for her father and stepmother and standing in for their departed mother for her siblings.

Alfredo was not a demonstrative parent. Occupied in the fields during the day and by rehearsals and concerts at night, he was very strict at home, where Rosa María had responsibilities both in the field as an earner, and on the domestic front, with daily housework and meal preparation. If Nelly felt the children performed a task inadequately or stepped out of line, she would insist that Alfredo beat them, which he did. The eldest Herrera sister was deliberate in using the word "beating" rather than "spanking" to describe the excessive punishment, which was consistent with Roland's recollections of their childhood and adolescence. In one of Nelly's particularly disturbing episodes of rage, she retrieved Pura's wedding dress from storage and set fire to the garment in front of the children—a searing example of Nelly's capacity for cruelty.

When Rosa María spoke of the many new responsibilities that accompanied the family's immense losses, her propensity was to look for the silver lining in the difficulties of their youth. "Sticking together" was a refrain she would reach for time and again to acknowledge that some good had come—*had* to come—from these hard times. Even though the children had lost their mother and experienced cruelty in their new household, at least they had each other and could grow up together, finding strength and comfort in being united.

Rosa María's quick conversational turn to silver linings also comes across in Herrera's memory in a story he shared on Facebook about the grade school tradition of exchanging cards and candy in class on Valentine's Day.

> When I was a child I would dread Valentine's Day at school. Kids bought and shared Valentine's cards, and it was a show of family income because some brought fancy cards. Some even had candy attached. We would have a party and classmates would put their personalized cards in the fancy shoe boxes we had decorated in art time. Because we couldn't afford cards, we either didn't go to school that day or we used recycled cards from the previous year that we had cleaned up the best we could. Worse, some sat and watched while classmates passed out cards. I was always relieved when the ritual was over. But I remember coming home and sharing the box of cards with great joy with my siblings who probably had the same experience. The cards were our entertainment for months.
>
> Still, love is beautiful and is the only way to our freedom.
>
> Happy Valentines day ya'll.
>
> Will you be my Valentine?[13]

Even though the classroom had been alienating, it was clear that Herrera had a broad sibling group to share the burden with at home: "But I remember coming home and sharing the box of cards with great joy with my siblings who probably had the same experience."

When speaking with Rosa María, one clearly discerns an image of brothers and sisters who were a refuge to one another in hard times. As a sister-mother, her determination to maintain an optimistic outlook likely played a role in how her younger siblings looked at the world; she applied her hopeful nature not only toward her own survival but toward theirs as well. We see this with Herrera's turn toward the joy the siblings found in each other, assuring the readers that his childhood self had sought and received consolation at home when there was none to be found at school. His post then switched to the second person, where he extended his soothing tone to his readers and offered to be their friend and companion at the post's conclusion: "Happy Valentine's Day y'all. Will you be my Valentine?"

The seasonal work the Herrera family performed kept them moving from place to place, and at times, they needed to miss school to help earn money picking fruit. Despite these significant obstacles on their educational journey, they managed to perform well academically. Roland couldn't recall a time when his parents ever read to him or helped him with his schoolwork, but even so, Alfredo vigorously insisted that they study hard and gain new skills in school. He remembered that their father would tell them, "You have to get educated so you can work in air conditioning. That's what you want to have."[14]

As it was in Texas, even though Herrera and his parents had been born in the United States, they were simply "Mexicans" in Oregon. In his 2016 interview with Elena Foulis, he recalled in a matter-of-fact voice, "We faced discrimination all the time." As a child, he learned quickly that speaking English and being articulate were rewarded, but he later acknowledged that these were ways in which he had been trying to assimilate or integrate into the society's narrow definition of "normalcy." Without a critical understanding of the ways in which Mexican culture and Tejano identities were being repressed all around him, it was difficult to name the internalized self-hatred that was the result of living in environments where White identity was prized and other cultures and histories were punished.

Herrera had not only performed the work of a highly skilled crop worker as a young child; he also served as a translator and mediator. In an interview with Josh Culbertson, he described how these responsibilities were crucial to his family in his early childhood.

> I was a child laborer. . . . And so my life, it seems like I've grown up pretty fast. Spanish was my first language. I learned how to speak English very well, very quickly, and when that happened, I think I was rewarded. . . . And then I became my family interpreter, and so that's a really interesting thing as a child at seven, eight, nine years old to be able to do that, people get paid for doing that right? Or they should be getting paid to do that. But I had the responsibility very young as a child and so I learned the dynamics of my family, of my father, and a lot of times I would interpret between him and the boss, and so I learned labor issues. . . . I learned how to negotiate those things and also how to negotiate the emotions because my dad wasn't always the most tolerant person, but I knew what triggered him and so I didn't want to do that as a son, as a child. . . . I learned mediation skills very, very quickly.[15]

In this complex reversal of roles, the parent depends on the child, and the child is the one who meets the parent's needs through caregiving behavior. Herrera had to learn how to convey essential information that could alter the employer's perception of his father and put the family's wages at risk. A simple misinterpretation could be disastrous for the family's pay or workplace experience, not to mention the frightening prospect of his father's anger. As Herrera noted, being a language broker was an adult-level responsibility. But that remark was again followed by the inclination to seek silver linings by assuring listeners how this difficult work also led to a set of social, emotional, and interpersonal communication skills that paved the way for his acuity as an organizer later in life.[16]

In interviews, Herrera looked back critically on the pressures he felt to assimilate to mainstream Anglo culture. "I wasn't Ru*bén*, I was *Ru*ben, right?" he noted in the Foulis interview. Although he did well in school, he was made aware that he was the "good one," an exceptional specimen in the vein of, "Why can't all Mexicans be like Ruben?" His English skills and his charisma were constantly on display, such as when he was put to work in local farmer's markets selling strawberries to English-speaking patrons, pulling heartstrings while hearkening back to the plantation fantasy of jubilant, dark-skinned workers. He witnessed a reward system that functioned at the expense of his siblings and other peers who each had their own set of gifts and aptitudes. But it was only the ones who moved toward the elite norm, and who were pleasing to Whites, that received encouragement.[17]

It was not until his last years in high school that he gained an understanding of how intersecting categories of race and class had unconsciously shaped him and instilled in him the drive to assimilate.

In 1973, just two years before Herrera graduated from high school, Chicano activists and organizers were determined to build an educational initiative that represented the unique needs of their community. Organizing to deter INS raids, the Willamette Valley Immigration Project evolved into Pineros y Campesinos Unidos del Noroeste (Northwest Treeplanters and Farmworkers United), referred to by the acronym PCUN. The first farmworker union of Oregon, PCUN sought to protect individuals from hazardous working conditions, unjust pay, and the ever-looming threat of deportation raids, but it also saw the need for wraparound services that would benefit the well-being of the entire community, including adult education, vocational training, day care, health services, and summer school for migrant workers and their families.[18]

PCUN's experiment in adult education brought a new and reimagined purpose to the failing Mt. Angel College in Mt. Angel, Oregon. Rechristening the school in 1973, the new Colegio César Chávez became the first and only independent, accredited, and degree-granting institution developed by and for Chicanos and migrant workers in the country's history. With a philosophy closely aligned with Paulo Freire's Pedagogy of the Oppressed, Colegio César Chávez created the "College without Walls," in which students were not expected to abandon work, family, and community life to excel as individual thinkers and scholars. Rather, they were allowed to remain attentive to the needs of their community, an acknowledgment that "they learn valuable lessons from their community experiences that can be brought to the classroom, as well as the fact that theory learned in the classroom can work toward solving community problems."[19]

A note is needed here about the impact of Chávez, Dolores Huerta, and the United Farm Workers, whose activism inspired the Colegio's name. This movement was not only the start of farmworker organizing on the West Coast but also served as the foundational development on which Chicano cultural identity was forged. With the UFW, campesinos (farmworkers) employed civil disobedience, hunger strikes, boycotts, picket lines, and other grassroots organizing measures to resist abusive labor practices and usher in a new era of pride and resistance. The cultural ripples of these events were felt throughout the worlds of art and politics: El Teatro Campesino ("Farmworkers' Theater") formed in 1965 to bring visibility to the needs of farmworkers during the five-year Delano grape strike and boycott in Central California. The poet Alurista's "El plan espiritual de Aztlán" articulated the seminal narrative of Chicano nationalism, in which it is declared, "We are free and sovereign to determine those tasks which are justly called for by our house, our land, the sweat of our brows, and by our hearts. Aztlán belongs to those who plant the seeds, water the fields, and gather the crops and not foreign Europeans."[20]

In sum, campesino advocacy, as a lingua franca of Chicano movement identity, brought Emiliano Zapata's creed that the "land belongs to those who work on it" north of the border. The United Farmworkers represented the struggle for farmworkers' rights but also the struggle for the dignity and determination of all Chicano and mestizo peoples. For Herrera, both the specific and strategic advocacy for the rights of agricultural workers in Oregon, and the symbolic advocacy that galvanized self-recognition of Chicano people beyond the fields, were formative and lasting influences.

At the tail end of the Chicano Movement (1965–1975) out West, Herrera and Roland were involved in the early organizing of Colegio César Chávez, helping to plan marches and occupy Mt. Angel College until Rubén's cohort of young students and the PCUN organizers achieved the goal of founding the "College without Walls." Herrera described the struggle for the Colegio as the origin of his "consciousness as a Chicano," the point in his life when he began to move toward, rather than away from, his roots. As he put it, "I started coming back to who I was." He regarded these years in the early seventies as a turning point, when he stopped thinking of his heritage, language, and color as deficits for which he needed to overcompensate, and he began to see them as integral to who he was in an unjust society that marked his community for exclusion.

In high school, despite being a straight A student and being in the National Honors Society, he had not been on an academic track for college preparation. Not a single guidance counselor appeared in his life who suggested college might be the place for him. Referring to Chicanos and Mexicanos, Herrera recounted, "What they did for us was they got us jobs."[21]

As a senior, he worked half-time for the Oregon Department of Transportation Highway Division—a welcome prospect compared to arduous agricultural labor in the fields. After his stellar academic achievements in high school, he went on to work full-time for the Oregon Department of Transportation for approximately eight years. It was during this period that he decided to enroll in an English class at a local community college, where something sparked in him. "Then I took another class," he said, "and I found that's where I needed to be."[22]

By the early twenty-first century, 59 percent of the population of Woodburn was Latino, a diverse combination of first-generation migrants and long-term residents.[23] The strongly Mexicano-Tejano-Latino environment provided a fertile atmosphere to maintain and grow the musical traditions that remained at the heart of the Herrera's social universe.

Alfredo helped to introduce one of the early, brass-infused orquestas to the region with his band, Fred and the Latin Americans. They often began their sets with "La cacahuata," a song featuring two saxophones.

Written by Luis Guerrero, the song was first released by the Sunglows in 1964, and a recent glance at the YouTube video of the infectious Sunglows' 1965 recording yields a touching post from Yvette Sanchez who writes: "I can remember my parents dancing to this back in the day, at Mission County Park, San Antonio, Tx. All the couples were dressed to the nines and the swish, swish of the tacones as they danced are seared in my memory! Thank you Diosito for making me a Tejana!"[24] An ebullient polka, the song's two saxophones seem to be in conversation about which one lives the sweeter life, with the deep walking notes from the electric bass settling the dispute by bringing everyone together to whirl in time on the dance floor.

In Tejano and Mexican musical traditions, even the melancholy songs that sound like sobbing will yield cathartic glee on a night out with family, friends, and romantic interests. Along with the Sunglows, some time listening to Little Joe and the Latinaires (who were preceded by Fred and the Latin Americans) provides a window into the emotive power of a Tejano orquesta. Little Joe's "Virgencita de mi vida" (Buena Suerte Records, 1968), for example, opens with a grito (yell), impassioned to the point of absurdity, that reminds us that crying and clowning need not be mutually exclusive on a night out. On YouTube, the song is recommended by one Emily Romero, who supplements her praise for the music with a dire message for the homie who dares to leave Little Joe off the setlist. "I love love love this musica," she writes. "Believe me when I say this while growing up in East LA in the 60's . . . with all carnalas and carnales . . . Little Joe was the ultimate to listen to and believe me if you did not have Little Joe, WAR or Oldies in your album collection you were screwed."[25] Emily Romero, looking out for fellow carnalas and carnales, wants everyone to believe her when she urges you to represent raza pride with Little Joe on repeat.

I, for one, believe.

The region already had some conjunto groups, but Fred and the Latin Americans were one of the earliest horn groups—a proper orquesta—that played to appreciative Cuban, Puerto Rican, Mexican, and Chicano audiences in Portland, Seattle, Tacoma, and other small and large cities throughout the Pacific Northwest.

Fred and the Latin Americans was a family band. Alfredo played saxophone, Roland played keyboards, Raúl played bass, a schoolmate of Roland's was on the saxophone, their stepmother, Nelly, would sing and play maracas, and Rubén, the youngest member, played drums. They played so frequently that at times it felt like a chore. If there was a get together at the family home, the brothers sometimes resented that they would have to pick up their instruments instead of enjoying activities of their own choosing.

Throughout the labor history of the United States, there have been many changes to the regulations surrounding children as laborers. The Fair Labor Standards Act (FLSA) of 1938 established the right to a federal minimum wage, required overtime pay for work performed beyond the forty-hour week, and prohibited the employment of minors in "oppressive" labor. However, the new standards provided for many exceptions in the area of agricultural work when there was parental consent, and they did not apply to minors employed as actors or performers in film, television, theatre, or radio.[26] Live music would have neatly fallen into the category of the sparsely regulated entertainment industry while also meeting society's general belief that benefiting from a child's earning potential was the natural privilege of parenthood.[27]

Labor performed by Herrera and his siblings saw them playing gigs deep into the night in adult-only nightclubs and other venues. While the surprising skills, talents, and charms of child entertainers impress audiences, the sacrifice the children make is not so easy to see. I think of this whenever I see an infant crying on a set for film or television. The child is crying in earnest; they did not take method acting classes to prepare for the scene. A baby cannot provide consent for the distress it clearly demonstrates, take after take, while on set, adults wield the infant like a prop.

Roland recalled that he had been a child performing in nightclubs when the family was still in Texas and that these were spaces where children were not normally allowed. The young Herreras were required to navigate the adult world of vice, sexual expression, and violence that they were still too young to understand. For Herrera, this included sexual impropriety, as both adult men and women took advantage of his innocence in the nightclubs.

According to the American Society for the Positive Care of Children, a report of child abuse is made every ten seconds. One in three girls and one in seven boys will be sexually assaulted by the time they reach eighteen. More than four children die each day because of child abuse, and 70 percent of these victims are under the age of four. Over 90 percent of child sexual abuse victims know their attacker, and approximately 30 percent of the victims of child abuse grow up to later abuse their own children in a vicious cycle of family violence.[28] Instead of protecting his children in these adult venues, Rita Herrera told me that her father believed that Alfredo played a role in the repeated abuse. Even though Herrera is no longer able to provide details about his father's actions, it was evident that Alfredo had not been sufficiently protective of his youngest son, who dutifully labored across many work sectors to keep the family solvent.

While some of the family members I interviewed were reluctant to raise this aspect of Herrera's childhood trauma, others felt certain that Herrera would have wanted this shadow world illuminated—not as a personal grievance or deferred vendetta against his father or Nelly but rather as another kind of labor issue to which so many children, both in the fields and in the entertainment industry, are especially vulnerable.

Despite the dangers, when the elder Herrera siblings spoke of their family's achievements, they were uniform in recalling the importance of music in their family, characterizing it as a source of cohesion and pride.

According to Roland, music was not just the family business; it also played a role in Herrera's introduction to Chicano activism. By the time he reached his high school years, Herrera had proven himself a stellar student with a clear talent for leadership. In his senior year at Gervais High School, he served as student body president while maintaining a job with the Department of Transportation and putting in many hours at Woodburn's Centro Chicano Cultural.

The Centro had been established in 1969, which followed the first Fiesta Mexicana in Woodburn that took place in 1964 and continues to this day. A heady time for Chicano public life, the late 1960s and early 1970s also saw the founding of the Valley Migrant League by activists. The organization provided bilingual services, a health care clinic, and organized childcare centers.[29] In sum, it was an energetic moment that saw many gains, and Tejanos contributing to the cultural life of Woodburn like the Herrera family were at the forefront of a new type of community activism that was not as prevalent in Texas.

As Luke Sprunger (2015) writes in his *Oregon Historical Society* publication, "In Texas . . . Latino leaders generally came from an elite business and professional class, were generations removed from migration, and had no experience with manual and seasonal labor. . . . Tejanos who settled in Washington County (and in the rest of the Pacific Northwest), however, were themselves migrants."[30]

Thoroughly relating to the struggles of immigrants, the migrant Tejanos of Woodburn could see themselves in the struggles of their Mexican-born neighbors and friends. Many of the early Tejano leaders were able to advocate for their struggle as Chicanos and Mexicanos more broadly, seeking long-lasting benefits for a diverse Latino population that needed to work together. This context gave the public-facing expression of Chicanismo—which bands such as La Ganga represented—an unparalleled significance in the making of a people.

In 1975, when Herrera was finishing school, Roland had already been involved in marches and was helping to organize for farmworker rights. He had also been trying to get Herrera out of his father's band and into his own.

> In those days the marches had their guitar players. We'd play "De colores" and songs like that. I was one of the guys with the long hair and the guitars and Rubén was right there with us. Next thing I know, he was going to all the marches with me, but I had a hidden agenda. I wanted him to be our drummer of the band La Ganga. It was one of the biggest bands here in Oregon at the time, it was like *the* band. I remember our drummer was sick and Rubén, who played with my dad, filled in. Afterward, all the guys looked at me and said, this guy has to be our drummer. It's like the Beatles when they got Ringo.

Members of La Ganga were excited to bring Herrera into their fold, even though it was a bit disloyal of Roland to have seduced him out of their father's band, in which he'd been a star drummer for many years. The two became close in the musical world of La Ganga, attending parties together as bandmates and close companions.

"At the time, the song 'Me and My Baby Brother' came out by War," Roland recalled. Even though he crossed his father to steal the prized drummer, the young Herrera was likely more suited to the youthful, long-haired, rebellious nature of La Ganga's performance style, which would involve going on stage shirtless at times and never failed to raise their voices and fists for the Chicano movement. "We were wild and crazy, like the early punk of the '70s—Chicano style."[31]

With long, tousled hair and sporting platform shoes, Roland and Herrera were at the forefront of a popular scene in the years they played and toured with La Ganga. They represented not only Tejano music's psychedelic side, but they also openly identified with the aims of the Chicano movement, in which farmworker's rights figured prominently. In one poster made by students, they advertised an event with César Chávez as the featured speaker. Sharing a billing with the activist at Colegio César Chávez, the poster read "Música Chicana, música con La Ganga" and introduced Chávez and the march as the top-billed event. The Herrera brothers both met with Chávez that day, and they would soon go on to increase their involvement in UFW protests.

On Chávez's campaigns, many locals were recruited to bolster his security detail and lend insights about the terrain. Chávez had very much been a target, receiving hate mail and threats as a prominent union organizer and more so as an advocate of migrant rights. Roland served in this capacity on a campaign that took him from Woodburn to Reed College in Portland and then on to Washington. At Chávez's side, Roland lent support and protection while learning valuable lessons about leadership and communication skills that would then animate many conversations he had with his younger brother.

Mesmerized by his eloquence and vision, the Herreras revered Chávez. Roland recounts a particular story about the ant and the elephant that Chávez would tell. In it, an elephant climbs to the top of a hill every afternoon at dusk to stomp on and kill the ants.

> All the ants got together and had this meeting. "Cuando viene el elefante, vamos a subir al arbol y cuando viene en la noche, lo brincamos." When the elephant comes, we'll jump on it. Like that's going to do anything, right? . . . They were going to organize and jump on the elephant. That night when the elephant went up there, he looked around and didn't see any of them. Then one of them says, "¡Ahora sí!" and at the signal, they all jumped on him.[32]

The elephant easily shrugged off the brave little ants and went right back to stomping on them. But one single ant had managed to cling to the elephant at the pachyderm's enormous neck. From below, the fallen ants raised their voices and cried out, "¡Ahóracalo! ¡Ahóracalo!" ("Strangle him! Strangle him!"). "The theme was," laughed Roland, "Don't ever give up."

The deep Chicanismo of this humor, not only as it reverberated in Chávez's story but also in Roland's ready laughter as he recounted it, made me smile.

We Were Very Young Parents

For Herrera, the mid-seventies were not only a time of Tejano music and the fervor of political awakening. It was also the time when he met and courted Thelma Sanchez (now Sanchez Murphy). Born in Reynosa, Tamaulipas, Mexico, in 1961 to Tomás Sánchez Sepulveda and Estér Sánchez Escobedo, the fourteen-year-old Sanchez Murphy met Herrera after he had finished high school in 1976. She had heard of his brother Roland through La Ganga, and she knew who Alfredo and Nelly were. Local celebrities, the two were hosts of a Spanish-language radio show in Woodburn. But she still had not met Rubén.

Throughout their teen years, Woodburn had a popular gathering place outside a movie house that featured Mexican films on Sundays. This was where Rubén and Thelma first met, when she was accompanying her sister who was on a date. At that time, Herrera's social life had the heady vibrancy, and plenty of the routine excesses, that came from being a young man in popular touring bands. Shortly following their first encounter, Sanchez Murphy spent time with Herrera and a friend of his, and she admitted they were drinking, a factor that contributed to the lightning pace of their romance. "That was a very young age to drink and it was something I had never done, but that's how I met him."

When talking about these early encounters, Sanchez Murphy seemed to work through latent pangs of self-consciousness or embarrassment that an adolescent typically feels when their parents catch them breaking the rules. Or perhaps, as a grandmother, she may have been reticent to share the type of socializing she engaged in that she wouldn't want her grandchildren to pursue. It made me think of the universality and durability of teen awkwardness when she described how she and Herrera had been children together, dealing with the adult-level implications of their new romance.

Like Herrera, Sanchez Murphy had been a field worker helping the family from an early age, but by the time she began to get to know the

Herreras, they were all employed in other industries. Herrera was working for the Oregon Department of Transportation. Alfredo worked for the DMV, Nelly was working as an assistant at a Woodburn school, Rosa María was married and living in a different household, and the youngest, Ruth, was still in high school.

The values of putting family first and helping the parents were clear, to the point that Sanchez Murphy had no idea what kind of wages she earned at her job: everything went to them. She recalled that by the time she reached adolescence, on the occasional Saturday, she was allowed to keep a day's wages for herself so that she could buy the kind of outfits she and her girlfriends craved. They all wanted to go to the weekend dances in style, which meant not wearing the clothes their mothers had picked out for them.

What did they want to wear?

"Bell-bottoms," she laughed. "The in-fashion bell-bottoms of the time. . . . We didn't get to choose our outfits, so it was that one time that we wanted to wear what *we* wanted. . . . I didn't feel like we were able to fit in until we were able to do our own shopping."

As with Herrera's father, Sanchez Murphy and her siblings needed to translate for their parents. Languages other than English were stigmatized, and she recalled being told not to use Spanish as a child, without having any idea about why English was imposed while her first language was discouraged at school. When her mother prepared lunches for school, Sanchez Murphy also didn't want to eat them around students who didn't share a similar background with her. "I was always embarrassed to eat in front of any friends or anybody who didn't know our culture," she said.[33]

One can picture the teenaged Herrera and the teenaged Sanchez Murphy in their swinging bell-bottoms, discovering they shared a history of adult responsibilities and each of them craving a precious moment of independence and playfulness against the austerity of received values.

Soon after meeting him, an unexpected package was delivered in the mail that turned out to be a gift from Herrera. The package contained a silver necklace with a pendant in the shape of a heart.

"That's what caught my attention," she said. "It was kind of like, 'Who's this guy? Why me? Why is he paying attention to me?'"

What began as curiosity about Herrera's attentions quickly gave way to a relationship that progressed faster than intended. "A couple times he came over to listen to some music in the living room. My parents were there and everything." But soon, another visit took place when her parents were on a trip to Mexico. Away from her parents' supervision, she traveled with Herrera to Eugene with her sister, and when they came back, she spent unsupervised time with him at Roland's house.

When her parents returned, they asked her if the two had had sex. Because the answer was yes, Tomás and Estér told their daughter that she could no longer live in the family home, and she was obligated to move and live with Herrera from that point on.

"So that's kind of how we ended up together," she said. Sanchez Murphy attributed the pace of their relationship to the traditional cultural values her parents held. "Not a virgin" meant that she no longer belonged to them: a daughter's first sexual experience constituted a breach in the family's contract to care for her.

Herrera recounted entering into their marriage in a similar light. When his teenaged girlfriend became pregnant, their parents strongly pressured the two to marry, even though they knew very little about each other.

"I ended up having a child at a very young age," he told Foulis. "I was like sixteen, right out of high school, and . . . my parents kind of forced me and . . . the mother of our child to come together. [We] really didn't even know each other. And then next thing you know, we had another child and then another. And so we were very young parents, and that was not so uncommon at all."

In my conversation with Sanchez Murphy, I asked her, "Did you feel too young to become a parent and get married, or did you feel like it was an expected thing for everyone to do?"

She replied that it had felt like it was something she was supposed to do and very much in the natural order of things. "Now it's your responsibility to get up and make his lunch when he goes to work," Nelly instructed her. She was still in high school when she found herself in the Herrera household with all of the responsibilities of a wife.

She had been pregnant with Ruben Jr. when they got married in 1978. Because she was still shy of the state's legal age, the two traveled to Vancouver, Washington, where she was not required to have a parent sign for her. When their second child was on the way, the two had only been together for a year.

"The day was exciting," she recounted. "I was still very young. I learned a lot from him. He probably became like a parent to me, just because I was so young."[34]

My next question to her felt indelicate, but I found myself wanting to know more about the emotional stakes of this whirlwind courtship that took place at a point in which their families and community still had so much influence in their lives.

"When you look back, were you in love," I asked, "or were you just following the paces because that's what you were supposed to do?" When I heard myself say this, I hoped my question hadn't offended her. On the contrary, she confirmed right away that, even though she had still been a child at the time, she and Herrera had truly been in love.

"His words to me when I was fourteen . . . he said, 'I love you,' and it melted my heart. It was not something I heard very much from my parents."

Even though their affection was genuine, she couldn't help but miss her own family. They were only about a twenty-minute drive away, but the drastic upheaval of her world was a shock, and she felt judged by her sister and four brothers. She had been the middle child, and suddenly, she was sent away, no longer a part of the family fold. The feeling was one of intense rupture and isolation. She did, however, find herself with a relatable group of young people when she was pregnant with their first child, Rita. Her high school enrolled her in a teen mother's program, where she befriended other expecting Latinas who came from families with similar values and expectations.

As one might predict, one of the main things the young couple tangled about was Herrera's late nights with Fred and the Latin Americans and La Ganga, and then with his next band, Los Rebeldes. Throughout the seventies, Herrera was consistently playing drums in Tejano bands. His activities would take him away until late at night and not infrequently into the next day. He also struggled to meet the emotional needs of a young mother and the demands of their infant children when he was still trying to figure out his own personality and priorities.

"He wanted to be free to enjoy some time alone," Sanchez Murphy said. At one point, when Rita was a toddler and their second child, Ruben Jr., was less than a year old, they lived in different apartments for a time, but they quickly reunited when Herrera discovered he missed them deeply and returned.

What was Herrera like as a father to Rita, Ruben Jr., and their youngest daughter, Naomi?

"He was a good father," Sanchez Murphy told me:

> He would tell them when things weren't right, and he would scold them. But he would turn around and make them laugh so that they knew things were alright. He always snuggled with them and told them how much he loved them. He communicated with them constantly, if by phone or by text or by email. I have nothing bad to say about him as a parent, he was great with them.[35]

One of her favorite memories of Herrera was the excitement the two shared many years later over the births of their grandchildren. She also lit up when remembering his joy when Rita was born and he first became a father.

"We weren't married then, so I wasn't under his insurance," she said. "[With] every paycheck, he would go to US Bank and make a payment on her." Herrera made in-person, steady hospital payments on the debt incurred to the hospital for Rita's birth.

"That's what I remember about that time of our lives. He said, 'I finally got her paid off!'"[36]

In the early 1980s, Herrera decided he no longer wanted to play in a band and became involved with the United Methodist Church in Woodburn. Methodism, or the Methodist Movement, is a Christian denomination with roots in eighteenth-century British Anglicanism. It's founder, John Wesley (1703–1791), along with his brother Charles Wesley and the Anglican cleric George Whitefield, brought new values to the Christian faith in England. The early founders broadened the audience of Christian ministry, and Whitefield, in particular, was famous for saying at the end of his sermons, "Come poor, lost, undone sinner, come just as you are to Christ."

Along with this revolutionary approach to evangelism, early Methodism emphasized the plight of poor workers. Its adherents established orphanages, advocated for the improvement of social conditions through charity and works of mercy, and formed small groups to support mutual edification. Over time, the early doctrine of predetermination shifted drastically to embrace an equal opportunity model of salvation. Known as the "four alls," Methodism holds that, "All need to be saved (the doctrine of original sin); all can be saved (universal salvation); all can know they are saved (assurance); and all can be saved completely (Christian perfection).[37] Today, the World Methodist Council (WMC), a formal network of churches in the Methodist tradition, comprises more than 40.5 million Methodists in 138 countries.[38]

Although he was baptized and received first communion in the Catholic tradition under the supervision of his Castilla grandmother,

Herrera shifted to the Methodist faith after finishing college. "I gradually became United Methodist," he recalled. "It was a time in my life that I was really in great spiritual need. I was lost, and I had nothing else." His older brother Rudy, who had by then returned to live in Texas, reached out to him and helped to ground him in prayer.

As noted previously, their uncle Chago and aunt Brígida had been instrumental in introducing the Herrera siblings to the Methodist faith. Their older brother Rudy went on to become Reverend Rudy Herrera, an ordained pastor at La Trinidad United Methodist Church in Seguin. Herrera described these days as being profoundly difficult, and he was overwhelmed by intense emotional pain and fragility. On the phone with Rudy in Texas, Herrera sought comfort from his older brother, who offered connection through spirituality and worship.

In retrospect, Herrera did not consider this to be a "now I've seen the light" moment in life but rather a turning point that took place when he decided to follow his brother's advice and look for a church after his career as a drummer in Tejano bands had run its course. Rudy's quiet wisdom was a sign pointing him toward the community of support that he had been lacking.

"I think part of faith is really a community of support that's healthy, right?" he remarked to Culbertson in 2017.[39] As migrant farmworkers, their ties to the Castillas had been abruptly severed, as was their connection to the parishes and familial networks that would have provided a sense of belonging that Herrera had long craved. His ties to the United Methodist Church in Woodburn quickly deepened, and he became a youth pastor. In that capacity, he traveled to the Philippines and Nicaragua with the church. Inspired by what he saw on his two-week trip to Nicaragua, his travels left a deep impression, and he knew he had to do more. Following these travels, Herrera was certain that he needed to commit to a life of service and progressive action. With his wife's encouragement, the couple decided he would go to school full-time while she continued to work.

Herrera was confounded by the fact that he had lived some eight or so blocks from Willamette University in Salem, Oregon, but never realized it was there. A prestigious, private university that Herrera described as "very elite," he was thrown into completely new territory when he enrolled and eventually majored in Spanish there. A father of three, he was one of the only Latinos in the entire student body. He felt that no one around him could understand his cultural background or working-class roots. Furthermore, his father and extended family did not know how to relate to him on this new path and were at a loss for ways to encourage him. His recollections provide a window into a familiar sentiment among students who are the first members of their family to attend college. "They didn't know what to do," he remarked in the Foulis interview.

> It became a lonely space because I started learning, and then there was no one to share that with when I went back home with my family, right. And my family were all very proud of me. But they never told me really. They would brag about me in their own spaces, but not to me . . . I wouldn't get that reinforcement from them. So it was very lonely. And I remember going up, there's a chapel, and it was a tall, older building and I used to literally always go out there and cry.[40]

Despite the isolation he experienced at Willamette, there were also opportunities to continue developing his consciousness as a Chicano activist, as when he again met and connected with César Chávez. Gathering with a small group of people for half a day, Herrera would describe the encounter as one of the highlights of his undergraduate years. He credited the meeting with Chávez with reinforcing the growing sense that he needed to be doing social justice work, but as was the case with many of Herrera's formative stories about his heroes and leaders, he also felt some disappointment when he asked the great visionary for his insight or advice about the struggle for farmworker justice. Instead of advice,

Chávez offered a simple comment, which Herrera was unimpressed by at the time: "It's not going to be easy."

Over the years, Herrera would grow increasingly grateful for the wisdom of this seemingly artless statement.[41]

Sanchez Murphy recalled another important influence in Herrera's life at that time. In his Chicano movement circle, he came to participate in activist organizing with Dr. José Ángel Gutiérrez. Gutiérrez taught at Colegio César Chávez in 1980, followed by a four-year stint at Western Oregon University in Monmouth. In Texas, he had led La Raza Unida, a political party organized around electing Chicanos to boards of education and city councils. He served as director of the Hispanic Services Project for the United Way of the Columbia, Willamette, and Portland area before eventually returning to Texas in 1986. Herrera took inspiration in the work Gutiérrez spearheaded in Oregon and worked with him on newspapers and posters, but he also quietly questioned Gutiérrez's leadership style, which seemed to him to be an overindulgence in ego.

Graduation from Willamette University with three children, courtesy of Naomi Herrera.

Herrera graduated from Willamette University on May 17, 1987, some twelve years after graduating from high school. Herrera was thirty when he finished college, and he and Sanchez Murphy were no longer the teen parents they had been in the seventies. From Sanchez Murphy's vantage point, Herrera had gone from being away from the family for long hours with various bands to being away from the family for long hours with his friends at school, but from Herrera's perspective, this was when he finally discovered his vocation and felt the need to tend to it with singular urgency.

It was at this point that Herrera received what he described to his wife as a calling, and he felt confident that the ministry was his life's true purpose. He received a scholarship and enrolled in the Methodist Theological School in Ohio, located in Delaware County, just north of Columbus. His system of beliefs and his activist organizing had long been closely intertwined, just as they had been for his paternal grandfather, Crescencio Herrera, in the Magnetical-Spiritual School of Universal Commune. It was not enough to fight for better material conditions for the poor—any path associated with the redistribution of resources had to consider the transmission of love and faith as well.

Shortly after the birth of their third child, Naomi, in 1983, Herrera confided another kind of awareness about himself to Sanchez Murphy. "He told me he was bisexual . . . and so he would go to the gay bars and would tell me things about how people talked, how they reacted." In these private conversations, Herrera acknowledged the judgment and social exile that, for far too many, accompanied the LGBTQ+ experience.

If Sanchez Murphy had fostered any judgment or concern about Herrera's orientation at the time, there was no trace of this in our conversation in 2020. To the contrary, she brought it up when she had been searching for the language to describe what he might have considered to be his most important achievements.

His circle process, or the amalgam of methods and intentions that Herrera's loved ones and broader community refer to as Trust the Circle, was a central aspect of his organizing during his years in Ohio. "I think, if he were to be able to go back in time to use this," she told me. "I think he could have made it bigger . . . it could have been used in the past had he known about it."[42]

It's important to note here that Herrera was not the first person in his family to identify as bisexual or gay. Roland remembered that his mother always doted on her younger brother Rudy, with whom she had been very close. Their tío Rudy had moved away from Seguin and lived in San Francisco: "He'd come from San Francisco, that's where he lived in those days, and he would always bring really cool gifts for us, little things . . . I always remember him wearing those sandals. But I didn't know he was gay till later. But you know, I mean, who cares, he was a great uncle."[43]

While their uncle Rudy had been a bit of a mystery to Pura's children, it would have been evident to her that her favorite brother lived a lifestyle that was more at home in San Francisco, California, than Seguin, Texas, and this had not prevented her from drawing him close as her favorite of the five brothers. Perhaps they were not open about his identity, but Pura extended unconditional acceptance to Rudy in their home and in the family's life.

Herrera's older sibling Ramón was born in January of 1952—the same year as Roland, who was born in December. Ramón Herrera had been in same-sex relationships from the time of the family's years in Texas, and he didn't make a concerted effort to conceal this from family and friends. Like Herrera, Ramón had been a stellar student and a natural in student body leadership. Ramón was the only brother who didn't take to musicianship, and when their father asked the boys what instrument they wanted for Christmas, his reply had been, "I want a telescope."[44] Even so, he accompanied the family bands to shows and on tour as their loyal roadie, and in the 1960s, Ramón seemed to have managed a way of carrying himself in social spaces that was both discrete and authentic:

> I kind of knew he was gay . . . but, man, everybody, everybody loved him. . . . [Rubén and Ramón] were both very brilliant. . . . They didn't come out until they were [older], but once Ramón came out, man, he was hardcore. . . . He'd go to bailes and in later years, he and his partner would go to Mexican dances with us. He didn't give a shit. He'd dance with my sister and stuff, he didn't go *that* far, but in those days, fíjate. He would support all my bailes. In fact, there were some guys who would say little comments to me, "Ah, there's your gay brother." You're goddamn right. Back then, estaba diferente, but I was real proud of him.[45]

Roland recalled that Ramón came out while serving as the first Latino student body president at the University of Oregon in the late seventies. Before then, Ramón had started a school newspaper at Woodburn High School that advocated for students' rights, which included a call for the rights of girls at the school to wear pants.

Once he was out of school, Ramón's aptitude for student leadership shifted to concentrate on the work of gay rights and advocacy. When the Oregon Citizens Alliance attempted to put statewide legislation on the ballot, which would have denied LGBTQ+ residents protected status, Ramón organized at the forefront of the opposition. Roland shared a memory of Ramón's determination and effectiveness in an article for *Keizer Times*. Each time the OCA held a press conference, Ramón helped lead the charge to make the LGBTQ+ presence known. The largest rally took place in Pioneer Square in Portland, and the brothers and fellow demonstrators managed to outnumber the OCA supporters. "We were fighting giants," Roland told *Keizer Times*, "but we were going to fight."[46] Ramón is remembered as one of Herrera's influences and a trailblazer in his own right: he was undeniably cut from the same cloth as the last ant on the elephant.

When considering Ramón's generation of activists, it's important to remember some of the details and high stakes that shaped the 1980s for LGBTQ+ communities. Gerry Studds of Massachusetts became the first openly gay member of Congress when he came out in 1983. In 1984, the Berkeley City Council passed a domestic-partner policy that extended insurance to city employees in same-sex relationships, making Berkeley the first city in the United States to provide benefits to same-sex partners.

However, the late seventies and early eighties saw the sporadic appearance of a previously unknown virus that became known as a "gay disease," since gay and bisexual men constituted an early primary group among the infected. The United States government contributed to the stigmatization of the disease by doing little to address or stem the epidemic, given that the virus was primarily affecting gay men, drug users, immigrants, and racial minorities.[47] On the world stage, Princess Diana made headlines when she shook hands with a patient with AIDS at London's Middlesex Hospital in April 1987—a shocking thing for most people to see. In other words, when Herrera first came out to Sanchez Murphy, he had a strong role model in his brother Ramón and an earlier family history of acceptance that involved Pura's creation of a loving space for her brother Rudy. Even so, the 1980s were associated with both significant gains and the extreme stigmatization and dehumanization of gay and bisexual people of color.

Herrera belonged to a family that defied clichéd expectations of Tejano and Mexicano masculinity. He was a family man and an activist. He was quietly queer and loudly Chicano. Underneath it all, he was driven to learn more about his new calling to pastoral service, and he was excited to begin graduate school at the Methodist Theological School in Ohio.

But before Herrera and the family could move to the Midwest, Sanchez Murphy made the difficult decision to leave what had become an unhappy marriage. At that point, Herrera obtained custody of the children, and he reasonably believed that his situation as a single parent of three meant that he would not be able to move forward with his plan to pursue a master's degree and a pathway to Methodist ministry. However, upon exploring his options, he learned the Methodist Theological School offered family housing and a supportive community for his children, and he decided to take a leap of faith.

"And I came," he said about his move to Columbus. "I didn't know anything, and I came with $500 in my pocket."[48]

Chapter III

BEYOND TACO BELL

Discovering the Columbus Model

> He started working with different minority groups and then it began changing and shaping him into who he ended up being. That streak had always been in him, but it all came out in Ohio.
>
> —Thelma Sanchez Murphy[1]

The thin, unproductive soils of unglaciated southeastern Ohio on the border of West Virginia are no match for the fertile loams found throughout the rest of the state. Their high agricultural yield is owed to the glacial deposits from the Pleistocene Ice Age that began a mere 2.6 million years ago. Lake Erie and the Ohio River, major sources for irrigation and transportation, were created by these receding glaciers, and the Holocene epoch that took place ten thousand years ago saw the resulting streams that have partnered with the geological clock to etch and excavate their imprint onto Ohio's verdant landscape.[2]

The first peoples of Ohio were primarily of the Erie, Kickapoo, and Shawnee nations. In the 1790s, when other Indigenous groups were violently forced into conflict or relocation by settler-colonizers, Ohio was one of the areas that received migratory waves of, among other groups, Lenape (Delaware), Miami, Ottawa, Seneca, and Wyandot. A series of unfair treaties led to the Ohio Removal between 1840 and 1845, and the Indigenous people who remained in Ohio after the removal and refused to go west were subsequently declared by the government to be "no longer Indian."[3] The denial of Indigenous peoples' existence and the deliberate falsification of their affiliations led to a situation in which presently, about half of the Indigenous Americans in the United States do not have identity cards issued to them.

As it was with the migratory waves of Indigenous peoples following forced relocations from other territories in the nineteenth century, White entitlement and xenophobia continue to define Ohio's mythology of who belongs and who does not, and the past decade has seen the state lurch into increasingly more extremist, antidemocratic, and reactionary directions. However, in the late eighties and early nineties, Herrera was no longer the school-aged family wunderkind who unwittingly sought assimilation. The seasoned activist who arrived in Ohio in 1987 already had many political and spiritual tools of resistance at his disposal to help him reconstitute his identity as a Chicano in the Midwest.

Ohio history and Latino identity have a rather complex relationship. In 1860, migrants accounted for approximately 14 percent of the state's population, and the few inhabitants of Latin American and Hispanic descent were concentrated in the major cities of Cleveland, Cincinnati, and Columbus, where they were chiefly employed in the industries of manufacturing and agriculture. Some of them would establish businesses that provided heritage products to the Spanish-speaking Ohioans, but a significant surge in population would not take place until the 1960s. By the 1980s, there were over 120,000 Latinos in the state, and as of 2019, estimates show a number closer to 470,000—4 percent of Ohio's total population.[4] While people of Mexican and Puerto Rican heritage make up the majority of Ohio's Latinos, Central America has increasingly become a more common point of origin.

And while statistics indicate the Latino population has tripled in Ohio since the 1980s, there are many factors that lead to undercounting across all ages and walks of life: hostility toward undocumented people, the lack of Spanish-language competency within the Census Bureau, fears of family separation among recently documented people, and a general mistrust of the Census Bureau and its representatives. If Spanish-speaking populations continue to be targeted for exclusion, census results will yield numbers that do not adequately reflect Ohio's actual demographic profile.

As a Chicano and a single parent of three, Herrera was most certainly an outlander in his new home. Methodism had been one of the earliest Christian denominations to arrive to Ohio, however, and his Methodist affiliation placed him squarely in a much larger fold in his new state. The prestigious Ohio Wesleyan University, for example, was established by the church in 1842—the same era that saw the violence of the Ohio Removal. When the university officially opened in November of 1844, it was one of the earliest Methodist institutions to be named for John Wesley, and European-American place-names proliferated in the ancient, glaciated spaces where Indigenous nomenclature had once sounded.[5]

Herrera pursued a master's degree at the Methodist Theological Seminary's Divinity Program, attending classes from the fall of 1987 through the winter quarter of 1989. His coursework, according to the MTSO registrar, would have covered subjects such as pastoral counseling, Old Testament studies, beginning Greek, Christian history, and Christian ministry. In his inquiry, he and his cohort were learning about how Christianity has dealt with some of humanity's greatest questions, which encompass the spiritual dimensions of injustice, suffering, illness, death, and grief.

Family tragedy was to strike very soon after Herrera and his children began their Ohio residency. Alfredo Herrera abruptly passed away in July of 1988, only one year after they moved to the Midwest. The World War II veteran, musician, radio broadcaster, community leader, and family patriarch suffered a heart attack in the garden of his home in Oregon and passed away at the age of sixty-seven. In my conversations with Herrera's older brother Roland, he held that Herrera had managed to make peace with his father and that the years had helped him shed the acrimony that accompanied a childhood of loss, loneliness, and frequent cruelty. The consequences of Alfredo's personality would continue to reverberate, however, as the siblings each harbored their own set of covert "undiscussables" that would contribute to a sense of isolation into their adult lives.

Ultimately, Herrera did not end up graduating with a degree in his program of study. Nor did he pursue ordination. From his track record, which is clear from the evidence of several interviews with his close relations, Herrera was valued deeply not only for his wisdom and kindness but also for his spirit of rebellion that was accompanied with a strong dose of belligerence: he resisted the doctrinal, "methodic" prescriptions of faith while at the same time embracing any and all communities that anchored charitable service and advocacy for the oppressed. Even if he energetically rejected modes of "magical thinking," or the notion that he had been "born again," he was also deeply spiritual, and he applied his training in pastoral care in many circumstances where this was needed.

Herrera's spiritually also took on decolonial forms, which he articulated through his observances of Día de los Muertos (Day of the Dead); Mexican Marianism, which sees the Virgen de Guadalupe as an iteration of Mexica (Aztec) earth goddess Tonantzin; and his lifelong respect for the spiritually charged curatives that his paternal grandmother had performed. Herrera would fully dedicate himself to providing action-oriented, community advocacy throughout his Ohio years, but he did this without stumping for a particular denomination or wielding a clerical credential for legitimacy.

As noted in the previous chapter, the cities where Herrera had resided in Oregon had sprung into action during the Chicano movement, but when he landed in Ohio, there had only been about 120,000 people in the entire state who identified as Hispanic and/or Latino. He remarks on this isolation in the Foulis interview, while making it clear that he wasted no time in creating new networks and collaborating on placemaking initiatives at every opportunity:

> It was 1987, it was lonely. . . . We as Latinos, in Ohio, wherever we are, we come into these spaces, and even though . . . we're educated . . . we're just thrown back into the question of who am I and why am I here, right? . . . I would come to Columbus, and I would look for sounds or smells or language. . . . But we find each other and there was a group of people that we met with . . . there was a coffee shop where we'd go meet.[6]

As his remarks indicate, Herrera was quickly intent on building a sense of community. He routinely gathered with a few Latino and Latina professors at the Ohio State University, and the small group decided to form the Hispanic Alliance of Ohio. He served as their first secretary-treasurer, which anticipated the many offices he would hold and the organizations he would spearhead in his new state of residence.

What were his early impressions of Ohio?

Arriving in the summertime, Herrera found it to be incredibly hot, with a level of humidity he had never experienced before. Along with the dearth of Latino heritage spaces and friendly faces, he had to acclimate to the sounds of tornado sirens and the details of severe storm watches that he needed to suss out.

Seeking restaurants that would offer the kinds of foods that his palate craved, he spent time driving around, looking for Mexican and Latin American fare with his children—this was before Google and Yelp—but they could find nothing. The establishment they finally landed on was the Taco Bell on High Street near Hudson, and they would go on to regard the spot as a family landmark, a place where they had to bear down and figure out how in the world they were going to the make this new place a home.

When the family moved to the Midwest, the children's mother and extended family were all back in Oregon. Sanchez Murphy recalled this as a difficult time but quickly saw that the children loved their new community in Ohio. "It wasn't just about me or him, it was about them." In my interview with Herrera's second daughter, Naomi Chamberlain, her early understanding of her parents' custody situation was that their father took the three of them to Ohio because he had access to more financial stability than their mother did. When asked if their family had struggled to pay for necessities in Ohio, Naomi replied:

> When we moved there, I remember him talking about how he was on food stamps, and just the struggle to feed us when we first moved to Ohio. . . . But then it shifted as he got into his career and got married. . . . There were times I remember asking for money. And [he would say], "I don't have any." I was like, "Oh, just write a check." Those are things that you don't know as a kid, and he was good at masking that.[7]

Naomi confirmed that, for the most part, they were happy in their new lives. Although she had been a young toddler when they moved, she recalled making the exciting cross-country trek in a Volkswagen bus and then arriving to a supportive community that had other kids she could play with, and families who helped Herrera take care of the children while he attended class.

When they moved to the Midwest, Rita was eight, Rubén Jr. was seven, and Naomi was three. The distance came with its particular set of difficulties for the separated parents, but despite some initial conflict around their parenting arrangement, they settled on the children returning to Oregon for summers and holidays. Rita moved back to Oregon when she was seventeen, and Naomi moved back when she was fourteen. Finally, Ruben Jr. returned as an adult around the time he married. Sanchez Murphy credited Herrera's second wife, Deb Garverick, with helping to maintain a loving and harmonious relationship with her children that encouraged their ties to Oregon and to their mother's love across distances created by time and space.

Although he was a practicing Methodist, Herrera soon realized that the Catholic Church was where people of Latin American heritage would gather in significant numbers in Ohio. At times, he attended Spanish-language mass to be in the same space as his community. As previously noted, the period between the 1980s and the present day saw the Latino population triple in size, and he was there to witness the steady expansion of Mexican-owned and Mexican-operated stores and restaurants on Columbus's West Side. The city's Hilltop neighborhood became an important destination for him to take in the market fruits, vegetables, and other offerings that he couldn't find anywhere else. Gradually, he began to discover the city's circuitry of food, language, smells, and sights—the sensual universe—that told him he was home.

Lincoln Park West Arson

If the 1990s were a time when Herrera forged cultural ties in Central Ohio, the roadmap for his activist practices was yet uncharted. Leticia Vazquez-Smith, who is originally from Mexico City, met Herrera around 1990. The two were invited by Rosa Rojas to a meeting with several other Latino residents of Columbus to conceptualize a new cultural organization that would help promote Latino culture and bring visibility to migrant oral histories. This project eventually became the Latino Immigration Stories oral history project. The group spent time interviewing individuals about their experiences, and Herrera was still heavily involved in the cultural aspects of Latino placemaking. He joined with Rojas and Vázquez-Smith to help found Latino Arts for Humanity, a Columbus organization that continues to host the citywide Day of the Dead celebration.

The first Day of the Dead celebration put on by Latino Arts for Humanity in Columbus took place as a small workshop in 1999, and Herrera would come and share in the festivities and community feasts. Cultural work was a priority for him, and he placed a special emphasis on spearheading conversations about what mattered to Latinos of Columbus. As Vázquez-Smith recalled, "The activist part wasn't there as much."[8]

In 2004, this would drastically change.

On September 12, 2004, ten Mexican migrants were killed at the Lincoln Park West Apartments, including three children. The fire, and its implications for Spanish-speaking migrants on Columbus's West Side, made a deep impression on what Herrera would make of his life in Ohio.[9] As he told Foulis, it was "something that happened that really changed my consciousness as an Ohioan":

> I heard in the news on Sunday morning . . . and nine people were killed. A family of five, mother, father and three children, and then some other people that were staying there. And they were Latino immigrants. I saw it in the news, and I decided that I'm going to go there to see what I could do to volunteer. . . . And I get there and it's chaos, and there's fire trucks in the snow . . . and the Red Cross, and there's a bus there housing people and it's a mess . . . people are in trauma. I went to the Red Cross, and I was probably one of the first Latinos to go over there. And I said, What can I do? How can I help? [I was] thinking they probably needed interpreters, but what they told me surprised me. They said . . . "People want clergy," and it reminded me that in situations like that, we go back to our spirituality.[10]

As it happened, Herrera had recently helped develop a book of resources that included Spanish-speaking businesses and churches. He had it on him at that moment, and it proved to be a helpful instrument to connect devastated community members and first responders to the kinds of assistance the victims sought.

Herrera soon learned that the fire had been caused by arson, which triggered several levels of local and federal government investigation. He quickly realized that not a single representative from any of these offices spoke Spanish. "Right away, I saw there was a need," he told Foulis. "Even the 911 call . . . the caller didn't know what to do." Valuable time had been lost in this cultural and linguistic confusion—valuable time that may have saved the lives of the family of five that perished. The local authorities ended up hiring a Cuban interpreter from Florida, whose dialect and culture were very different from the fire's survivors, the majority of whom were of Mexican background.

At that point, Herrera was already a valued presence at the forefront of Ohio's Latino community. He had been awarded the honor of Distinguished Hispanic Ohioan by the Ohio Commission on Hispanic/Latino Affairs in 1991, and he received the Distinguished Latino in Central Ohio Award given by the Columbus Crew, the city's professional soccer team, in 2004. While these accolades were an obvious measure of his success in bringing the needs of Latino Ohioans to the attention of regional policymakers, the events of the Lincoln Park West arson compelled him to acknowledge that Ohio's newest Spanish-speaking denizens required a different level of advocacy, agency, and healing that was not yet on Columbus's administrative radar.

Though he arrived in Ohio as a seasoned activist and no stranger to public-facing responsibilities, it was painful for Herrera to realize that he found himself speaking on *behalf* of Spanish-speaking migrants more than he was speaking *to* them, and he noticed that after years of college and graduate school in the States, his Spanish was different than theirs.

He also felt he had not been prioritizing the interpersonal aspect of advocacy; he had not yet developed relationships that brought him closer to the people he wanted to speak with, whose lived experiences he needed to be not just an advocate but also a full-fledged community member. In the Foulis interview, some of his sentiments were self-critical about ways his privilege of platform resulted in his own name recognition, while the wider community he endeavored to empower remained in the shadows.

Herrera's endeavors to build cultural spaces were paired with employment positions in the field of education—work that was closely aligned with the prospects of young people and the transformative power of education in the years that his children were going to school. These efforts were followed by his increasing urgency to bridge the space between his individual access to local and state institutions and the pressing issues Spanish-speaking, working-class Ohioans were facing.

Love Languages

Before looking at the work Herrera did, it's necessary to understand the family bonds he built that were at the heart of what made him an Ohioan.

People who are seeking relationship advice are probably familiar with the concept of love languages. It was developed by Gary Chapman's 1992 book, *The Five Love Languages: How to Express Heartfelt Commitment to Your Mate*, and it has been adapted and modified to suit an array of mainstream vernaculars that describe what the heart wants. Chapman theorizes that everyone has a dominant behavior, or one of five "love languages," that they most immediately associate with affection and caring: compliments, quality time, receiving gifts, acts of service, and physical touch. For a single parent, particularly in a new city far from kinship networks and community connections, any proverbial language of love needs to include not only paying attention to one's romantic partner but also attending to the vast spectrum of needs presented by one's children as well.

Deb Garverick was born in Newark, Ohio, in 1951. Herrera's second wife, she was kind enough to talk to me about the years she and Herrera shared when he, Rita, Ruben Jr., and Naomi had just arrived in Ohio. When I asked her what drew her and Herrera to each other, she immediately replied, "The way he interacted with children. His own, and . . . the children in my classroom, which I have a great love for. He . . . was a natural with kids. He was a big kid himself!"[11]

The two met after Garverick took a job in Ohio's Orange County School District in Delaware, where Methodist Theological School in Ohio was located. She began her new position teaching fourth grade in the same school year that Herrera and his children moved from Oregon. Wanting to become involved in Rita and Ruben Jr.'s new school, Herrera sought out volunteer opportunities and was assigned to Garverick's fourth grade classroom to help implement the Project Charlie initiative. Ostensibly a drug prevention program, the project focused on the broader goal of helping children develop self-esteem through dialogue skills around diversity and respect for difference, which was a solid fit for the issues Herrera had been emphasizing over the past ten years of his life. Garverick and Herrera also turned out to be a solid fit for each other, and the two were married at the end of 1989.

Married for over six years, Garverick and Herrera welcomed their daughter, Marisa Garverick Herrera, into the world in 1990. Reflecting on these years, Garverick looked back fondly on the time they shared. She described a trip they took to Niagara Falls and a visit to an exhibition in Toronto—destinations that middle-income families in Columbus could reach in a one-day drive. Likewise, Garverick's parents lived about an hour's drive from their home. In Ohio's sweltering summers, her parents' swimming pool was a big draw for a family with four children.

The Herrera children remember their father as being loving, devoted, and wildly playful. His daughter Naomi recalled Herrera as someone who created a loving home environment in which he brought his entire focus to their moments together. When they were young, Herrera would throw "slumber parties" on the living room floor with blankets and pillows. As they laid together, he shared stories from his life that were sometimes fun, sometimes sad, but all of them were offered with unreserved affection and provided them a sense of who they were and where they came from.

"We would laugh, and we would just sleep together. And it was just such a good foundation of connection and just love," recalled Chamberlain.[12] Herrera's son Ruben Jr. also remembered these living room campouts fondly.

> We would basically camp out in our living room and all sleep on the floor. I can't imagine what it must have felt like for my dad now that I'm an adult and sleeping on the floor sounds terrible.... Now that I have kids, especially with the smaller ones, ... when I hold them tight, I love giving them kisses. I feel like, "*This* is my dad."[13]

Each of Herrera's adult daughters provided memories of their father at his memorial service on April 13, 2019. No amount of paraphrasing could do justice to how they voiced their remembrances, so selections of their remarks appear in the book's final section to keep their own language and perspectives as intact as possible.

In my conversation with Garverick about her married life with Herrera, she demurred when I posed some of the more intimate, complex questions about marital conflict. She estimated their separation and divorce had taken place in 1996 or 1997. Clearly, they faced a set of insurmountable obstacles as a couple whose marriage ended in divorce. I hated to stir up any painful memories or to pressure Garverick (or any of the respondents who participated in this biography, for that matter) into saying something ungenerous about a loved one whose loss was still an open wound, but I also knew I needed to ask the occasional impertinent question to understand more about Herrera's life. Therefore, I was glad that Garverick let me know a couple times during our conversation that there were details she would be keeping to herself, and I sincerely hoped I hadn't come off as a pushy journalist-type on the hunt for the kind of "hot goss" that propels sales of celebrity scandal magazines.

Even so, when we think about the life and love languages of Herrera, we can't avoid acknowledging that the personal is, in fact, political. This is a fact any feminist woman of color or BIPOC queer family member who can't spend the holidays with their biological family knows all too well.

Garverick eventually offered some insights about her and Herrera's struggles as a couple that demonstrated how their family life was not immune to some of these dynamics:

> I think a relationship obstacle was that I was White. And that, you know, he was living kind of in a White world. . . . My family, for example. I mean, there could be things that were said or done that, you know, not meaning to be hurtful, that probably were. . . . Sometimes he would point things out, and . . . I would be like, gosh . . . I didn't see that. . . . I'm not familiar with that kind of thing. So, I think that was a challenge to be, you know, married to a White person [who was] just living in a White world. . . . Subtle things. And probably other things in your face, things not so subtle.[14]

As previously noted, the 1980s saw a demographic surge in Ohio's Latino population, but demography is no guarantee of an attendant shift in cultural awareness or interpersonal communication skills around sensitive issues of race, class, gender, and power. As Herrera and Garverick demonstrate, a couple that initially met over the common goal of introducing skills around diversity and inclusion in the grade school classroom were not impervious to the wounds of cross-cultural blind spots.

From Anti-Defamation to Immigration Reform

In terms of his career pursuits following his withdrawal from seminary school in 1989, Herrera's resume quickly reveals common threads across the professional positions he held. Herrera served as regional coordinator for the Anti-Defamation League's (ADL's) A World of Difference Institute, and between 1990 and 1996, he was the Ohio/Kentucky/Indiana point person for the implementation of the ADL's diversity and prejudice reduction program.

From there, he became executive director of City Year Columbus from 1995 to 1998. A member of the AmeriCorps national service network, City Year is a nonprofit organization focused on mentoring young people of all backgrounds to improve educational outcomes for higher-risk communities. Concentrated poverty in urban neighborhoods leads to significantly lower high school graduation rates (nearly 22 percent lower) and less state and local funding. And in a country with deeply rooted and systemic biases, concentrated poverty, along with family income, race, language, and gender, were also predictive of student success rates.[15]

Between 1999 and 2009, Herrera's resume states that he worked primarily as a consultant for Herrera and Associates, a group that specialized in community development and provided planning, vision-building, and diversity and inclusion strategies, and convened "conversations that matter" for activist organizations. Although this final "conversations that matter" language is explored further in the following chapters, these three words anticipate a larger matrix of practices and trainings that Herrera helped introduce to the Ohio activist community, and they are likely what he was alluding to when he spoke to Foulis of the "Columbus model" in 2016: "Latinos in Columbus are interesting, because . . . I think we were modeling the Columbus model," he told Foulis. "We say we're in the Westside, Northside, but there's no real density."[16]

As Herrera noted in the interview, Ohio's capital has several neighborhoods where specific nationalities predominate, which lends them a thematic and cultural unity; there are German, Italian, and Scandinavian Villages that each have their distinctive attributes and flare. Columbus's Latinos, on the other hand, were widespread around the city, and their presence was not attached to the nomenclature of any of the city's districts. They simply did not figure at the forefront of the city's image of itself. And even though Hilltop on the West Side can be said to have a stronger concentration of Spanish speakers, there are also other places around the sprawling city—usually identifiable by no more than a few Spanish-dominant grocery stores, the occasional brick-and-mortar restaurant, and one or two food trucks—with higher rates of Latino residents.

If the notion of "dispersion" does not, at first blush, seem like much of a "model," Herrera's circle-oriented approach was even more significant for creating a centering opportunity each time Latino organizers and allies came together. In the coastal city of Los Angeles, Spanish and Mexican history, proximity to the US-Mexico border, and steady waves of migration help Latinos there maintain strong ties to Mexican and Latin American identity. Manhattan likewise houses generations of Puerto Rican communities in diaspora, their entrenched struggles and prospects reverberating in the edifices of El Museo del Barrio or the Nuyorican Poet's Café. But Columbus, by contrast, was a place with no Latino monument or mythology.

The circle, as a device, became Herrera's practice that placed every individual who arrived to it at the center, and it turned community members toward each other in a gesture that hailed their intrinsic monumentality as human beings. The circle provided a way to dispel the sense of decenteredness for Columbus's Latinos and facilitated empowerment in a way that upheld the possibility of equal participation and universal inclusion.

Despite persistently participating in Latino civic leadership and advocacy for marginalized youth in his first twenty years in Ohio—through the A World of Difference Institute, City Year, and Herrera and

Associates—a consistent self-criticism running through Herrera's work on immigration reform in the early aughts was that his interventions had largely taken place at the "grasstops" level. In the Foulis conversation, he discussed how much of his work involved exchanges with lawmakers, donors, and people with influence. Nationally recognized as a civic leader, Herrera was chosen to visit Washington, DC, around 2003 with a small group of fellow Latino leaders to discuss immigration reform. "I went to Washington for a week or so [to] strategize with leaders from all over the country on [what] we were doing. . . . And so we were working on immigration reform . . . and that was a great struggle." Although he felt that what they were doing was important, "What *didn't* happen," he said, "Was that we were . . . not really on the ground organizing people. Like I said before, change happens when the people themselves understand who they are and why they're here, and the struggle emerges from them."[17]

To understand Herrera's diverse approaches to immigration reform, I spoke with Nicholas ("Nick") Torres. Born in Lima, Ohio, on Cinco de Mayo in 1985, Torres met Herrera while he was an undergraduate at the Ohio State University around 2006. At the time, Torres had been double-majoring in Spanish and international studies at OSU, and he held an internship with the New Americans Initiative under the direction of Guadalupe Velasquez, a leading figure across multiple organizations that provide services to new migrants and refugees in Columbus. The New Americans Initiative was a project commissioned by the Columbus City Council, in which OSU's College of Social Work was responsible for conducting a needs assessment in the city's human service landscape that included a range of volunteer services that were available to Ohio's newest residents from other countries. When Torres began attending community conversations related to the project, he quickly became fascinated by Herrera's skill for fostering dialogue.

An early conversation Torres witnessed had to do with decisions that Latino leaders needed to make regarding the citywide Festival Latino. "I know that there was a conversation about Festival Latino in

Columbus. I think at the time they were shifting the venue," recalled Torres. Founded in 1996, the annual late-summer celebration brings together Latinos of all nationalities with food, music, workshops, and Latino-owned and Latino-serving organizations and businesses, and Torres found himself at a meeting discussing the need for a new festival venue. There were clear tensions around how changes to the festival would affect the community.

> There were thoughts about bringing in law enforcement and there were thoughts from . . . grasstops leaders from the Latino community, and thoughts about how they're charging admission. . . . I remember thinking at the time, I had no idea what I wanted to do, but it was the first time I was [seeing] Latino community leaders coming together and having a conversation with so much different expertise . . . and just the way that he facilitated group conversations. Whether it was the Art of Hosting or a similar style, I found it fascinating and inspiring.[18]

Along with Guadalupe Velasquez, Torres included Ramona Reyes and Ezra Escudero as community catalysts who held prominent positions in Columbus's Latino-serving arenas of social services and public policy and who were part of leadership circles such as the one he witnessed related to Festival Latino. Torres was excited to be part of these conversations and to meet a new cast of characters who had clearly been at the forefront of Latino leadership in Columbus for many years.

In terms of immigration reform at the national level, Herrera's campaigns in Ohio placed him on an extremely consequential timeline. The year 2006 was particularly notable in the history of immigration issues. In December of 2005, Representatives James Sensenbrenner (R-Wisconsin) and Peter King (R-New York) sponsored the Border Protection, Antiterrorism, and Illegal Immigration Act of 2005. Known as the Sensenbrenner Bill, the act passed the House of Representatives by a vote of 239 to 182. Among other measures, it sought to criminalize violations of federal immigration law; increase penalties for housing and employing undocumented residents; shift immigration enforcement to state and local law authorities; expand expedited deportations; and expand the definition of "aggravated felony" to include the misuse of passports or other travel documents, even if that was done by a refugee or a victim of domestic trafficking.[19] The bill did not pass the Senate, but it was the catalyst for far-ranging mass protests in 2006. It also led to renewed debates about immigration in which a broad swath of migrant, social justice, religious, and human rights organizations joined forces to denounce the bill's measures.

In 2006, the issue of immigration reform remained a key focus of regional and national lawmakers, and the Senate passed the Comprehensive Immigration Reform Act of 2006 (CIRA), which was sponsored by Senator Arlen Specter (R-Pennsylvania) in May of that year. The act would have given amnesty to a majority of undocumented residents and was designed to increase the number of guest workers through a "blue card" visa program, which would provide more pathways for legal immigration into the United States. Although CIRA and a parallel bill (HR 4437) passed in their respective chambers, neither bill became law because the two houses were unable to reach an agreement to go to a conference committee. The 109th Congress (2007) saw to the defeat of both bills.[20]

Barack Obama's 2008 campaign had emphasized a strong commitment to immigration reform, and after his inauguration in 2009, the national Reform Immigration for America (RIFA) campaign was funded and organized by a large coalition that included unions and civic organizations that wanted to ensure immigration reform remained a priority on the Obama administration's legislative agenda. In 2009, the campaign was hiring organizers, and Torres joined as a grassroots organizer in December of that year.

Despite Herrera's reservations about performing grasstops advocacy, Torres and others encouraged and finally convinced Herrera to join the

RIFA campaign early in 2009. Herrera proceeded to take on the role as the campaign's state director in the following year. While Torres worked on bringing community members into the campaign and garnering strength in numbers, Herrera was responsible for galvanizing support among community leaders and policymakers. These efforts included organizing events to gain visibility and make shows of strength, such as holding candlelight vigils and other types of mobilizations to keep immigration reform in the headlines.

In February of 2010, Herrera sent out a letter informing people of his acceptance of the state director position, and he described the group's objectives: "The campaign connects people from communities across the country who are ready to work together towards achieving the 279 votes needed to win just and humane comprehensive immigration reform legislation: 218 votes in the House of Representatives, 60 votes in the Senate, and one signature from the President."

As state director, Herrera called for reform around issues such as the visa system, the pace at which immigration courts were reviewing cases, and protections for migrant workers surrounding wages and other workplace issues. However, after his experience with the Lincoln Park apartment fire, Herrera was someone who wanted to engage with people in a way that saw them as more than data points. He grew increasingly frustrated by the bureaucratic instruments of change that tied their success rates to rote boardrooms and signature cards rather than their ability to foster an authentic and intimate exchange with community members about their lived experiences.

By spring of 2010, it became clear that the nation was heading into the midterm elections, and, once again, comprehensive immigration reform was not going to be at the forefront of the policy-making agenda. However, there were notable offshoots that grew out of the RIFA campaign. The DREAM Act, for example, emerged at this time, and many of its principal architects had been involved in RIFA to varying degrees.

After Herrera stopped representing Ohio with the RIFA campaign at the national level, he and his collaborators continued to organize for immigration reform under the auspices of the Ohio Action Circle (OAC). Torres noted that, along with Herrera and himself, Florentina (Tina) Staigers was the most heavily involved member of the group, as was Guadalupe Velasquez in the organization's early years. Originally called the Latin@ Action Circle, the group finally settled on the Ohio Action Circle as their name. They had been inspired in part by Ori Brafman and Rod A. Beckstrom's *The Starfish and the Spider: The Unstoppable Power of Leaderless Organizations* (2006), which calls for open and shared models of leadership while pointing out the pitfalls of centralized, coercive leadership. "Centering ideology" was at the top of the meeting notes dated October 27, 2009: "Through an open system of deliberate, purposeful and intentional conversation we will address and confront anti-immigration sentiment, the dehumanization and criminalization of immigrants, racial injustice and all legislation that encourages this ideology."[21] Torres recalled that the group's centering ideology was a text Herrera returned to and adjusted fairly frequently, always searching to revise and sharpen the language and help the group develop as a site of open and continual reinvention.

In the "Centering Ideology" statement on the OAC's blog, the group maintains that immigration reform is tied to human rights, peaceful coexistence, and collective prosperity. It also points out that the appreciation of diversity is key to making the world a more just place. In terms of their commitments, they state:

> To ensure a more prosperous and welcoming state, we will continue to educate all Americans about the contributions of immigrants and empower immigrants to integrate, contribute, and thrive. We will continue to: Confront ideology and policies that encourage anti-immigrant sentiments and racial injustice; Support diverse leadership with collaboration, inspiration, active listening,

> and creative communication; Be proactive in preparing for federal immigration reform that upholds family values, protects American jobs and builds our economy.

Dedicated to acknowledging the contributions of migrants, confronting anti-migrant and anti-refugee sentiments, and encouraging and training diverse leadership in the skills of communication, the OAC maintained the goal of immigration reform at the federal level. The Action Circle's national partners included the National Day Labor Organizing Network, United We Dream, DreamActivists.org, Church World Service, the United Methodist Rapid Response Team on Immigration, Presente.org, Puente, the Georgia Alliance for Human Rights, Dona Tierra, Libro Traficantes, and Immigration Equality.

Herrera was invited to discuss his views and actions on immigration on the WOSU radio show *All Sides with Ann Fisher* on several occasions over the years. A recording from January 7, 2010, introduces him as "The Latino Action Circle Community Development Specialist/Community Organizer Rubén Castilla Herrera." On Herrera's resume, he described his role in the Ohio Action Circle as "Organizer/Catalyst," alluding to his responsibility as a leading convener of the circle as both an organizational shape and a co-creative and open method of shared decision-making: the Columbus Latino model in action.

The OAC group kept organizing in the community around deportations, the DREAM Act, and the rights of DACA students. DACA, or the Deferred Action for Childhood Arrivals program, protects eligible migrants—those under the age of thirty-one who came into the United States before they turned sixteen—from deportation and grants them work permits. Affecting approximately seven hundred thousand undocumented denizens who arrived in the country as children, and subject to renewal after two years, the 2012 Obama-era initiative was a temporary and limited opportunity for relief that was intended to help school-age young people who were struggling for inclusion and a path to citizenship in their homeland.[22] Related to DACA, the Development, Relief, and Education for Alien Minors Act (or the DREAM Act) allowed undocumented migrants to stay in the country legally as long as they went to college or joined the military, and provided a pathway to permanent residency. Introduced in 2001 by Senators Dick Durbin (D-Illinois) and Orrin Hatch (R-Utah), the proposal did not pass. But the DREAMers, those youth who were affected by the potential legislation, participated in activist interventions to raise awareness of and demonstrate support for the new law, and a movement emerged and began to gain momentum.

According to Herrera, this momentum helped some young people gain a new sense of self-esteem and agency, and he hoped to see it evolve to become more resilient and sustainable. "It has to emerge from the struggle," he noted, "And for the people that are struggling, I can do what I can to help. But [when] it becomes real to the people, whether they're women or young people [who] are DREAMers, then that's when things happen. That's exactly what happened with the DREAM Act. I think of Dreamers across the country, and here as well, [who] said . . . Why can't I go to school?"[23]

We should again qualify here what it meant for Herrera to throw his weight into a fight for policy change. While his public remarks supported Obama's executive action to create and implement the program, in his view, DACA was never enough. A decade later, DREAMers still struggle with anxiety and daily uncertainty, and they are unable to fully execute plans for their careers, lives, and relationships because of renewal requirements and their associated lengthy delays. Under the program, DACA recipients are only allowed to travel outside of the country for "humanitarian, educational or work related reasons" with advanced permission.[24] And this does not even account for the crush of migrants who fall outside of DACA's narrow parameters, which apply only to college- or military-bound young people. What of their parents, grandparents, and siblings, whose skills, aptitudes, and ethics took them in different directions? Herrera's full-throated avowal was reserved for the grassroots momentum that the DACA program helped inspire, and he hoped to see others take inspiration from the new energy and courage of DREAMers to cultivate a culture of pride and agency for all migrants, not just the ones deemed admissible by the program's exclusionary logic.

By 2012, a quarter century had passed since the intrepid Herrera had made that initial leap, in which he and his three children—like astronauts conducting a spacewalk, connected by thin tethers in an expanse of darkness—blindly stumbled into a Taco Bell on High Street in Clintonville. Beginning with educational and cultural initiatives, he evolved to become one of Ohio's most outspoken voices for comprehensive immigration reform. He responded to Columbus's decentering lack of dialogue, visibility, and sense of inclusion by developing an action-oriented circle practice: A place where all participants could listen and learn from each other, and where every voice mattered.

Chapter IV

DÉJAME CUIDARTE, DÉJAME ABRAZARTE

A Queer Latinx Elder in Columbus

Before the errant admiral sailed the ocean blue; before Indigenous lands were dispossessed and First Peoples were subjected to genocide, culturicide, and ecocide; before Native place-names were silenced by waves of settler colonizers and before territories became known by the names of their invaders; before Christianity's hetero-patriarchal values cleaved a new world order across the geographic and cultural terrains of the Western Hemisphere, the binary construal of gender had not been the universal law of the land.

Across the pre-conquest Americas, diverse regions were populated by cultural groups with vastly different ways of thinking about sexuality. California's Indigenous peoples maintained a culture of three genders: male, female, and joya; the Mexican muxes, assigned male at birth, dressed and behaved in ways that associated them with women; and First Peoples of the Great Plains had established the category of the "berdache" ("two-spirit") that applied to males who did not fit the standard characteristics of masculine behavior and who engaged in sex with other men.[1]

Today, "two-spirit" is widely used in the English language, but this term, which also conserves the notion of duality, is not always a satisfactory translation for the gender diversity articulated across many Native languages of the Americas. According to Brayboy (2017), at the point of contact with Europeans, many Native American societies acknowledged three to five gender roles: female, male, two-spirit female, two-spirit male, and transgendered.[2]

As such, European invasion and conquest also constituted, among other types of violence, a form of "gendercide," or the destruction of entire categories of gender in order to impose the nuclear family structure defined by heterosexual matrimony, the rigid control of sexual drives, and the repression of the body and its senses.[3]

This is not to say that homophobia and heteropatriarchy were nonexistent among First Peoples. Diversity, rather than homogeneity, defined the genderscape. In pre-conquest Mesoamerica, the homoerotic Maya paintings on the walls of the caves of Naj Tunich in Petén, Guatemala, demonstrate that the Maya were reasonably accepting of same-sex male relations. On the other hand, the pre-Cortesian Mexica (Aztecs) were extremely intolerant of homosexuality, even though many iterations of gender fluidity were played out across the theatre of their religious spectacles. For example, the Mexica warrior goddess Coyolxāuhqui is depicted wearing the male-defined warrior's regalia to lead her brothers in an attack against their mother, Coatlique, and during the annual feast of the grandmother goddess Toci, a male priest would pull the flayed skin of a captive woman over his own body to incarnate the grandmother-warrior deity in what had to have been the drag ball with the highest shock value in the history of the Americas. In order to discipline and curb the pursuit of same-sex partnering, conquest-era Nauhuatl (native Mexica) codices, followed by Spanish chronicles, make abundant mention of it, though this just provides ample evidence of its preponderance.

Today, Mexican culture continues to resist heterogenous thinking about gender and sexuality. Since August 2010, same-sex marriages performed anywhere within Mexico are recognized by all thirty-one states, but 2019 marked a deadly year for the country's lesbian, gay, bi, and trans people. The murder rate among those populations was 27 percent higher than in the previous year, demonstrating that legislative protections are no guarantee of safety from other practices of discrimination and aggression.[4]

Contemporary Mexico's spectrum of attitudes toward masculinity and sexuality reveals a widespread presence of a kind of male bisexuality that allows men to retain heterosexual status and privilege despite occasional, or even routine, sex with other men, provided they are the dominant partner in the coupling and they are discrete about their activities. In other words, the range of what falls within the parameters of heterosexual behavior is broad enough to include same-sex activities for male partners who assume the penetrative role—as long as they keep this behavior hidden.

This attitude of tacit acceptance, combined with social silence, was present in the Herrera family. In conversation with Culbertson, Herrera remarked that even though he saw his older brother Ramón as a role model, sexual identity was not discussed openly. When Herrera visited Ramón in college, he was able to take in signs around his house that led him to conclude his brother was gay, and Herrera felt that he "lived his gay life through him."[5]

It's important to note that even though Ramón had been out in other circles, the family gag order around the issue of sexuality remained strong, even when the two brothers were alone together. Sexual experience of any kind, recalled Herrera, was simply not discussed among members of their family. Let's not forget that even though Herrera could hold his older brother Ramón up as a proud, queer Latino and an agent for political change, Ramón's sexuality had to be downplayed in the Tejano family environment ruled by their oppressive father. And while Ramón was an outspoken leader in school and later in civic life, the family would also see him succumb to an early death in 1994 as a result of complications from the AIDS/HIV pandemic that was fueled by homophobia and discrimination: a stigmatization that led to extreme public fear and right-wing attacks.

Queer Latinidad in Columbus

In 1984, Columbus lawmakers at city hall considered an ordinance that would bar employers from discriminatory practices based on sexual orientation. Douglas Whaley, a law professor who helped draft the 1984 ordinance and testified in its favor, predicted that these public displays of homophobic sentiments would become, "As silly a matter as discriminating against blacks or women."[6] However, the AIDS crisis was in full swing at the time, adding to the ammunition conservative clergymen used to attack the proposed legislation. Declaring that homosexuality was an "unclean practice," and that employers would be forced to hire people who would spread incurable diseases, one of the conservative preachers lamented:

> I can't believe that the great city of Columbus is considering the passage of a bill of this nature. I believe if we pass it, it'll give Columbus a bad name. Homosexuals from surrounding states will flock here. . . . Who in the world wants Columbus to be known as the gay capital of the Midwest?[7]

Happily, this is exactly what came to pass. In 2015, a Gallup poll revealed that 4.3 percent of Columbus's population identified as lesbian, gay, bisexual, or transgender—a larger percentage than New York City. In 2010, the *Gay/Lesbian Index* listed Columbus as one of the top twenty "gayest" cities in America.[8]

Across several measures, the city was far ahead of the rest of the state. "Columbus has been holding, for instance, the Pride Parade since right around 1981, 1982, and other cities in Ohio have just hosted their first Pride festivals in the last few years," notes Eric Feingold, curator of the Ohio History Connection.[9] Having grown to be the second-largest Pride Parade in the Midwest (behind Chicago), organizers of the event can expect to see crowds of 500,000 people. With Democratic leanings, a robust nightlife, and major universities, Columbus's bustling Short North, German Village, and Merion Village are affluent neighborhoods that house the highest numbers of out, same-sex domestic partners, and rainbow flags can be seen in some of the most trafficked retail corridors as well as places of worship.

However, even while the rainbow flag is displayed in shops, businesses, and homes in prosperous neighborhoods, its colors are no guarantee of a community's commitment to the inclusion of non-White members of Columbus's queer communities. In the Culbertson interview, Herrera emphasized that, from person to person and from culture to culture, queerness has its own levels of diversity, issues with equity, and languages of safety and love to tend to. For him, the rainbow flag did not seem to signal inclusion, for example, of the Somali Muslim population, or of the city's undocumented residents who had other issues of visibility and acceptance to contend with.

"There are levels of complexity . . . you cannot possibly have just one space," he told Culbertson. Then, softening his assertion, Herrera added a note of characteristic ambiguity. "Or maybe you can. I don't know, I think we're still kind of playing with that."[10]

The dynamic of "coming out," as Herrera often noted in interviews when discussing the issues of visibility and safety, could never be a "one and done" prospect. Instead, it was a series of signalings, conversations, and declarations that were made across many social situations and over many phases of life. If there had been a furtive admission to Sanchez Murphy during their youth, there was also a new wave of heavy discretion that pervaded Herrera's first years in Ohio as he found new footing as a father and then as an advocate for Spanish-speaking communities contending with the pressing issues of immigration and access to basic public services. As such, there were many moments of disclosure and concealment before Herrera would enunciate his identity as an "openly out" genderqueer Latinx leader in Ohio.

Coming Out: Never a One-Time Thing

> Love takes off the masks we fear we cannot live without and know we cannot live within.
>
> —James Baldwin

In talking about his own discovery of his sexuality, Herrera told Culbertson, "I think I probably knew by about the sixth or seventh grade."[11] He recalled having affectionate feelings toward a school friend of the same sex, and they would walk down the hall together almost touching. It was not something that Herrera would have sought to act on at that age, but he was aware that this deep friendship was accompanied by an attraction—that mysterious range of emotions and vibrations that compel you to desire closeness.

In between his marriages to Sanchez Murphy and Garverick, he recalled furtively visiting gay bars in Columbus. He described it as putting a toe in the water but withdrawing it again quickly: too cold! In those early forays into queer spaces, he anxiously hoped he wouldn't "see anyone." The prospect of happening upon someone he knew from the world of his professional acquaintances or his children's school was uncomfortable to him.

In his conversation with Culbertson, he estimated that about 20 percent of the general population was genderqueer, but that this was "a little harder to see" in Latinx communities that didn't tend to meet in White spaces.[12] In those early ventures into LGBTQ+ establishments, Herrera reminisced about a queer Latino bar called La Barca (since closed), where Spanish-speaking and Latinx people could gather (along with White people who were attracted to them). Herrera called it an "interesting sociological experiment": queer spaces of color were on the "down low," and this culturally situated desire for discretion lent itself to a speakeasy atmosphere. He confessed that he missed those spaces where people could be true to themselves and cultivate a space of safety, free from the sensation that mainstream, corporate culture was trying to swallow them whole.

The rainbow flag, preponderant in Columbus spaces inhabited by Whites and people with socioeconomic privilege, was not a symbol that Herrera could see being used to galvanize working-class migrant and Black communities, many of whom belonged to churches or parish communities that marked them for exclusion. Herrera rejected the "we love you, but not your sin" attitude that characterized much of mainstream Christian thinking. Recalling his years of training in Methodist divinity studies, and how he had turned to Catholic mass as one of the initial places where he could connect with other Latinos, he was highly aware of the important role that Christian values played in either building—or hobbling—a sense of self-esteem for members of the queer community. Queer, working-class spaces for Black, Indigenous, People of Color (BIPOC) seemed to offer empathy for these shared corridors of exclusion and provide affirmation in unspoken ways.

Culbertson, who is White, told Herrera that when he arrived in Columbus, he believed it to be a very open and affirming city. However, after many conversations with queer BIPOC community members and allies, Culbertson learned to recognize his own blind spots related to his privilege in White-dominated LGBTQ+ spaces. In a gesture of critical self-examination, Culbertson confessed this early bias to Herrera.

"You know," he said, "my first reaction, I'm ashamed to say this today . . . was to get angry at you because I saw you as one of the people supporting and advocating for them and I saw that I was angry at them as individuals. I was angry because . . . why did you want to stop my parade? . . . I couldn't see it."[13]

By "parade," Culbertson wasn't speaking metaphorically. He was speaking about a literal action taken by the coalition of queer and trans people of color who, on June 17, 2017, peacefully disrupted the Stonewall Columbus Pride Festival and Parade. The four young activists—Wriply Bennet, Kendall Denton, Ashley Braxton, and DeAndre Antonio Miles-Hercules—would come to be known as the Black Pride Four. Their aim had been to draw attention to anti-Black and anti-trans violence that was on the rise. The day before the Stonewall Columbus Pride Parade, Jeronimo Yanez, the St. Anthony, Minnesota, police officer who fatally shot Philando Castile at a traffic stop one year earlier, had been found not guilty on all counts. Additionally, the group called attention to the number of trans women of color who had been murdered in 2017, a number that had reached fourteen by the month of June.[14]

In sum, the Culbertson conversation pointed to significant ways that, for Ohio Latinos, there was more at stake than whether the Pride Parade moved along at its usual pace. To his credit, Culbertson owned his ignorance and acknowledged that his awakening was owed, in part, to the courage of the Black Pride Four and Herrera's outspoken support of the bold actions they took to claim public space for their cause.

As Herrera emphasized in his interviews, coming out is a layered and gradual process of developing compassion for the inner self and then making a series of judgments about how and when to extend this truth to circles that may include family, coworkers, and a broader constellation of community members that make up one's social fabric. Given the preponderance of discrimination and prejudice, and the leadership position Herrera held among Spanish-speaking Ohioans, it's not surprising that family members and different members of his community have varying recollections and experiences regarding his process.

But first, it's important to acknowledge that the onus of "coming out" burdens LGBTQ+ folks with a "before and after" timeline that heterosexuals are simply not required to deal with. The origin of the "closet" as an expression for hidden or repressed gay sexuality passed into pop culture in the United States in the 1960s. Before then, the notion of being "out" referred to wealthy families whose debutante daughters made a public debut of their charm and beauty in lavish "coming-out" balls. Links to these cultural rituals raise questions about how queer folks are required to pronounce and explain their identities publicly—another way that nonheterosexual lives are marked as "other" in a heteronormative society. Do straight people have to worry about when and if they are safe enough to express an attraction? And what do the conspicuous consumption and competitive excesses associated with ball culture have to do with people inviting others into their truth? This can be even more acute for people coming out at a later age because they can be made to feel shame for not having been "honest" or "courageous" enough to live an authentic life sooner. Moreover, today's growing societal acceptance of gay, lesbian, trans, and queer identities has lowered the median age for coming out (more than half of gay men surveyed in 2013 said they had come out to friends and family before their twenties). This means that older LGBTQ+ people will often feel stigmatized for "taking so long" to invite family and friends into their truth.[15] Aware of these dynamics, in both the Culbertson and the Foulis interviews, Herrera makes note of the fact that he came out later in life—and he did not apologize for that.

Sanchez Murphy, as we've seen, was privy to Herrera's sexual orientation before the couple split in Oregon. However, Herrera would wait until his children were adults and out of the house before he chose to discuss it with them. He estimated his coming-out unfolded roughly between the years of 2000 and 2005, and he offered that his role in the Latino community in Columbus played a part in how he handled his identity.

> What happens when you are actually in love with another person of your own sex? What do you do with that? And a lot of it has to do with where society is at, right? And then culturally where you're at, because I'm Latino, Hispanic, and we may not be exactly

> where mainstream White queer community is, in general. All of that is going through my personal psyche while I'm trying to live and survive. So finally, I decided to embrace it, and I think it came out, it's been probably a good fifteen or twenty years now. . . . It's not like you're born again . . . it's just another level of consciousness, and the struggle continues in different ways.[16]

Above, Herrera took care to note, "We might not be exactly where mainstream White queer community is," emphasizing that different activity spheres and community circles required different levels of thoughtfulness. By this time in his life, he had come to be a spiritual elder, a community organizer, and a public voice for Latino Columbus. He had come to mean something to the city's Spanish-speaking circles, who knew him as a family man with Christian values.

Another message that Herrera would repeat about coming out as an elder was his commitment to the integrity of his family life. "The sexuality thing," Herrera told Culbertson, "was kind of hidden . . . while I was a father, and I don't regret that. I don't apologize for that space."[17] His children were young when he came to Ohio, and he knew what it had been like to grow up without a mother. Married to Garverick, and with Sanchez Murphy in Oregon, he focused on his parental responsibilities. One can imagine that it must have been no small victory for Herrera to have welcomed a stepmother into the lives of his three children who in no way resembled or emulated the cruelty he had experienced with his own stepmother, Nelly.

On the other hand, in spite of Herrera's repeated insistence in public-facing interviews that he did not need to apologize for his timeline and actions, his youngest daughter, Marisa, acknowledged that there had been some feelings of abandonment when, following his second divorce, Herrera placed more emphasis on his social life than he had done previously. "He did apologize to me in the sense that he didn't always show up in the ways that he wanted to show up for me. . . . And I really believe in simultaneous truths. I believe it to be true that he felt remorse for the ways that he hadn't shown up as a father . . . but also no remorse for finally being happy and being in a relationship that made him feel like his most authentic self. I think both of those things were definitely true."[18]

Even with the enormous triumph of providing a healthier and happier homelife for his children than he himself had received, there had to have been an amount of self-denial taking its toll on his psyche. Reflecting on this period later in his life, he confessed that he had not only kept his sexuality in the shadows, but he had also taken a turn toward a display of superficiality in general. Unconsciously, he found himself attaching mainstream, midwestern ideas about the nuclear family to middle-class materialism, where outward appearances held sway and governed his day-to-day life. My interview with Vazquez-Smith corroborated Herrera's description of the social skin he wore throughout the 1990s. "When I first met him, he was always in a business suit," she recalled.[19]

When I spoke with Herrera's eldest daughter, Rita, she felt that part of his struggles in his marriages with their mother and stepmother were due, in part, to the repression of his sexual identity.

"What was it like for you and your siblings when he came out?" I asked her.

"For me, it was like, 'That makes sense.'"

She estimated she had been eighteen in 1996 when Herrera spoke with her directly about this aspect of himself. When they were growing up, the children saw their father enter into close friendships with different men that he clearly cared about, but it was never addressed in conversation. "He was always hanging out with the outcast, the queer, the different people. And when he talked, he was very open, [saying,] 'Oh, that guy's cute.' Girls too, but he didn't shy away from saying that men are cute as well. There were hints there as a kid, so when he did come out, it was it was just like, 'Yeah.'"

After their father shared that he dated and loved other men, did she feel that was something they needed to keep to themselves? Had it been a private one-on-one moment, or did she feel it was something she could openly discuss?

"That's a good question," Rita replied. "I think he was 'out' when he said it out loud. But he was kind of already out in a way, before he said the words to me. I think by the time he said the words, he was getting comfortable with saying them and being that."[20]

I posed similar questions to Herrera's daughter Naomi when I met with her via Zoom in the spring of 2022.

"What was it like for you when he came out? How did he broach the topic of sexuality with his kids?" I asked.

She recalled a conversation with her father that had taken place circa 2001. Although his revelation was not a surprise to her, the topic had felt taboo to speak about until that moment. To her, this made it feel like it was an area of his life that was too sensitive to broach, so it was a relief to her when he finally told her himself. She said:

> When I was eighteen, he and I, we went out clubbing and we just had the conversations [about] when he knew of his first love when he was a kid. It was good! It was a good connection and understanding of who he was, and I accepted and was proud of him. . . . And so him telling me and really opening up and being vulnerable . . . It shifted my mindset.

After speaking with Rita, Ruben Jr. (who was also told when he was eighteen), and Naomi, it was apparent that Herrera felt it was important to wait until his children were older to broach the topic of his sexual identity in unambiguous terms. While they each felt that this was something that had already been hinted at and alluded to, when he finally invited them into a conversation about who he loved, they each conveyed a sense of relief: a window of honesty had been opened and the shadow of secrecy had been dispelled.

Radio Trancazos: The Last Frontier

Already in a same-sex relationship and out to many, for Herrera, his announcement on a Spanish-language radio show in 2014 seemed to serve not as a first coming-out moment but rather as the final threshold he needed to cross to eliminate any ambiguity about who he was and what he stood for. He described this moment in 2014 as the moment he decided to be "openly" out.

For context, Foulis had asked Herrera to name some of the difficulties he had faced in his life in Ohio. After Herrera related the Lincoln Park Apartments arson event, he went on to speak about another time when he struggled in his life as a Latino activist in Columbus.

"Yeah, let me throw something else out there," he told her. "I came out as a gay Latino male probably about fifteen years ago. . . . I don't have regrets about my children or my marriage, it was a beautiful moment and . . . I honor that, but I realized there was something else. As a community leader . . . (and I don't adhere to the leader model) . . . I decided to be openly out. . . . I decided to be on this radio show."

Already two years into his relationship with Pasquarello, Herrera was invited to be a guest on the Spanish-language Radio Trancazos. The host, Alma Rosa, started off by saying that Mexico was observing a Día Contra la Homofóbia ("Anti-Homophobia Day").[21] She asked Herrera, "Y tú qué piensas de eso?" ("And what do you think of that?").

Herrera took the opportunity to announce his identity as a gay man on that program, and the host was quick to share her emphatic support. They both agreed that Latino and Latin American communities needed to be more accepting of gender diversity, which was an area she acknowledged needed work. When describing the Trancazos interview to Foulis, it was clear that Herrera saw it as breaking down of the final barrier by asking the Spanish-speaking world of Ohio to accept him: a family man and a man of the people who was unafraid to speak his truth.

"Ice Ain't Shit," with Nicholas Pasquarello and Rubén Castilla Herrera. Courtesy of photographer Katie Forbes.

As mentioned in the introduction, the word "Latinx" has gained traction over the last decade. Just as there had been a thrill of excitement when Herrera and Pasquarello showed up in my class that winter day with members of the CIW (he liked my hat!), their presence in 2016 at the Onda Latina Ohio open mic night that I've hosted in Columbus since 2013 was an exciting treat. At Onda Latina events (changed in 2022 to Onda Latinx), nervous first-time performers are welcomed to share their unedited poems, which are often read from cell phone screens, alongside seasoned veterans playing original compositions on guitar. While I try to feature a Latina as the special guest, all are welcome to the open mic, and no one is left out.

In 2016, Herrera gave a totally unprepared and spontaneous sharing from the soul on the Onda Latinx mic. That particular gathering had taken place at Ethel's Left Stage Lounge on Columbus's major High Street thoroughfare. There are no recordings of his spoken piece, but I remember he talked about being a Brown man on "pinche High Street" where he had so many times stood in protest. For the uninitiated, in Mexican slang, "pinche" is the rough equivalent of "shitty" or "fucking." His words flowed with passion and rebellion, and he repeated the sentiment several times: he was a queer Latinx on pinche High Street.

What a delight.

—

Nicholas Pasquarello has been introduced in this book in a number of places already, but in Herrera's timeline, this is the point at which he entered his life and changed it forever. I met up with Nick and his partner, Edwin Woolever, at the Columbus home Nick had shared with Herrera starting in January of 2017. We spoke over pizza, salad, and a six-pack of Modelos while Nick and Edwin's two dogs vied for attention. Woolever was restoring the old home, and it was touching and delightful to see abundant signs of new life in a place that had borne the weight of so much loss in the preceding years.

Pasquarello was born in Phoenixville, Pennsylvania, in 1989, and he estimated it was the winter of 2011 when he met Herrera for the first time. At the time, Pasquarello was an upper-level student at the Ohio State University, majoring in psychology and sociology. He was also the co-president of United Students Against Sweatshops (USAS). In one headline-grabbing action that had taken place during his senior year, several USAS members went shirtless (women wore sports bras) to emphasize their opposition to a recent apparel deal Dallas Cowboys Merchandising had made, proclaiming they "would rather go naked than wear Dallas Cowboys Merchandising Apparel."[22] Marching between the Ohio Union and Bricker Hall, USAS took issue with the apparel company: the Institute for Global Labour and Human Rights had shown that the company was doing business with the Style Avenue factory in El Salvador, a known sweatshop. The institute's report detailed the conditions for the women who sewed there: they were paid seventy-eight cents an hour, or ten cents for each fifteen-dollar infant or toddler onesie they made; they were locked in a factory where temperatures frequently exceeded one hundred degrees Fahrenheit; they worked mandatory nineteen- to twenty-five-hour shifts when garments were scheduled to be shipped to the United States; sixty-hour weeks with mostly unpaid overtime were the norm; drinking water and dirty bathrooms were unhygienic and unsafe; and verbal abuse was constant.[23]

A measure of their solid reputation at the forefront of Columbus progressive activism, USAS would occasionally see Herrera show up to their demonstrations. USAS members also participated in other campaigns around the city that shared similar goals, such as the Student/Farmworker Alliance (Pasquarello founded OSU's chapter) and Ohio Fair Food. Pasquarello recalled it was early in 2011 when USAS participated in a national unionization drive for Sodexo employees. Sodexo, a campus dining subcontractor, offered services at the major athletic complexes such as the Ohio State Stadium and the Schottenstein Center, the respective homes to Ohio State football and basketball in a place where college sports are the core of the city's identity. It was at a Sodexo-related campaign, as both Herrera and Pasquarello were picketing outside of the Columbus City Schools Office, that they both remembered sustaining a more-than-casual glance across the crowd for the first time.

In January of 2012, Pasquarello came out as "bisexual." On social media, he changed his profile from "interested in women" to "interested in men *and* women." Within a day or so of this online shift, he received a message from Herrera, who invited him to coffee. There were a few exchanges and cancellations before they finally met with each other at Kafé Kerouac, an unpretentious coffee shop located just north of the OSU campus and a couple short blocks from where Pasquarello lived at the time. Herrera was living in Olde Towne East, over five miles away from the coffee shop, but he implied that he spent a lot of time there. The two started to meet up under the casual rubric of, "Yeah, sure. We should totally [meet]. . . . We're organizers, that's what we do."[24] They began to see each other at Kerouac and other places, at times involved in protest actions together and at times not.

In January of 2012, they were united again in organizing an action involving immigration rights. Yanelli Hernández-Serrano first entered the US alone at the age of thirteen, and she lived in the Columbus area for close ten years. At age twenty-two, she was placed in detention and ultimately deported to Mexico, despite the thousands of supporters around the country who held actions and contacted US Immigration and Customs Enforcement (ICE) to prevent her deportation. Hernández-Serrano suffered from mental illness, which led to multiple suicide attempts while she was in detention, and the process of deportation would undeniably place her at more severe risk for self-harm.[25] In their capacity as leaders of Reform Immigration for America, Herrera and Nick Torres enlisted USAS to help organize a candlelight vigil outside the OSU Student Union. USAS members joined the vigil, and Pasquarello and Herrera's planning meetings and coffee house visits culminated in a distinct rapport that they both recognized to be the beginning of something.

"Stuff happened," said Pasquarello, describing their evening after the vigil. He merrily pulled out one of Herrera's journals that he had in his home and, using his lawyer's lingo, opened it to a page that he described as the "time stamp" of when they began to be more than casually acquainted: January 29, 2012. In the journal, Herrera had scratched out a few shorthand notes following their first morning together, such as the word "ska" and the name of the band the Slackers—notes that tell the story of a fifty-something Brown man who is interested in a college-aged White man. It was a fully sympathetic page of musings that most of us could relate to, the homework one must do when trying to make a connection with a new romantic prospect.

For both of them, it was the first same-sex relationship they were involved in that had a public-facing aspect. According to Naomi, her father had been close with a man named Brian Johnson, who attended the Methodist church that held the first memorial service for Herrera after his death. "Dad never said they were a couple," Naomi said, but she looked back on some of her greeting cards from that time, and she saw that they were signed by both her father and Johnson.

Leticia Vazquez-Smith, like Herrera, was a longtime leader in the cultural life of Latino Columbus. The two had been close friends since 1999, and she also remarked that Pasquarello had been the first relationship that was associated with Herrera's public work as an area activist and organizer. "When he was with Nick," Vazquez-Smith stated in our interview, "that's when he turned into a butterfly."[26]

"Things went fast," Pasquarello recalled. But even though they both shared a profound connection, their early days were not wholly untroubled.

Their relationship was something that they kept to themselves for the first several months. Pasquarello recalled sneaking Herrera into his room so that his roommate would remain unaware of their activities, and Herrera had some trepidation about being associated with a much younger man, particularly considering the fact that he was already a prominent figure in Columbus.

As I talked about this with Pasquarello, he held out Herrera's journal to me. Herrera had sketched a diagram about where each of them were and where they were headed. The drawing indicated that the month of June meant that Pasquarello was going to graduate from college and leave the Midwest. Pasquarello wanted to move away from Ohio and had set his sights on California. Herrera's diagram showed that he, on the other hand, would be staying put: his life was in Columbus.

In June of 2012, Pasquarello moved in with Herrera, and those early "what do we mean to each other" conversations (and notebook illustrations) gave way to the mutual understanding that they were inseparable. On

February 1, 2019, Herrera wrote a tribute to Pasquarello on the occasion of their seventh year together on his Facebook page:

> February—7 year anniversary month—Aniversario de 7 años
> "Déjame cuidarte, Déjame abrazarte.
> Déjame enseñarte todo lo que tengo pa' serte muy feliz
> Que nunca nada te haga falta a ti.
> Te voy amar hasta morir."

Central Ohio Workers Center (Centro de Trabajadores de Central Ohio)

The respondents who provided their thoughts on Herrera for this book agreed with Vazquez-Smith's "butterfly" assessment of his life with Pasquarello. When Herrera met and partnered with Pasquarello, he entered into the full expression of a healthy and loving relationship. He made a point of not apologizing for who he had been before or for who he had become. This was something Herrera took care to emphasize: he was not examining his previous life through the lens of judgment and deficits. He was not the less-than-real Rubén before and then finally the real Rubén after: each part of his journey involved his whole self. At every step of the journey, he showed up to his life with the knowledge he had at the time, and he invited people into his truth when it felt it was the best time to do so.

It's important to understand how Herrera's perception of his responsibilities as a Latino leader was one of the factors driving his cautious approach to being openly queer. But there was another aspect of his decision to be open about his relationship, which had to do with the often unsung but absolutely vital impact his partnership with Pasquarello had on the causes and campaigns Herrera would champion after their relationship started.

While it was apparent to all who knew him in the last decade of his life that Herrera had found his soulmate in Pasquarello, it wasn't readily apparent that he was also able to pursue his deepest calling to finally move closer to the city's most vulnerable community members as a grassroots, rather than a grasstops, activist. This section brings some of Pasquarello's contributions to light and shows how his partnership with Herrera spanned both personal and political spheres.

In the Foulis interview, after covering several questions about Herrera's childhood, education, and the path that led him to Ohio, she asked him where his current energies were directed. He took the opportunity to discuss the Central Ohio Worker Center (COWC) and the reason they felt the need to create the organization.

> We knew that we want to start a workers' center, because a lot of the immigrants were low wage workers and actually have rights as workers, even the undocumented workers. We have somebody at the Worker Center that's working as a restaurant worker. . . . He's working to organize restaurant workers. He's been talking to . . . people who work sixty, eighty hours a week with no overtime, right? And, and there's lots of wage theft and then they're not paid, but certainly they're working those hours. So the Worker Center became a place where or people could organize or could be represented. . . . We do wage theft work, but also represent an immigrant community.[27]

Worker centers are different from unions in significant ways. Labor unions are an important force in the workplaces of the United States, negotiating for fair wages, benefits, and safe working conditions on behalf of their members. With a history dating back to the Knights of Labor in 1869, early unions brought workers of different religions, races, and genders together around their shared circumstances as workers. Representing more than twelve million active and retired workers, today the American

Federation of Labor and Congress of Industrial Organizations (AFL-CIO) brings together over fifty legally recognized unions that represent groups of workers in their collective bargaining with management. The issues they address include wages, health care and retirement benefits, working conditions, and contract disputes.

Worker centers, on the other hand, are nonprofit, community-based organizations that provide support for low-wage workers. These workers are often immigrants, and they seldom have access to the collective bargaining process and are often excluded from federal labor laws. With foundational principles in the tenets of international human rights and US civil rights, worker centers provide leadership development, legal support for wage-theft claims, and educational programs about workers' rights, which often address the issues faced by migrant workers whose prospects for self-advocacy are jeopardized by compounded forms of exploitation.

Early worker centers were organized in the late seventies and early eighties by Black worker activists in North Carolina and South Carolina, by Asian workers in New York City's Chinatown, and along the US-Texas border in El Paso in response to worsening conditions in manufacturing work. This was followed by a second major wave that took place from the late eighties to the early nineties, as large new groups of Central American and Southeast Asian immigrants joined the labor force and developed new models based on the first wave's strategies for grappling with economic exploitation.[28]

According to Janet Fine, the third wave began in the 2000s and continues to the present day. Resulting, in part, from an AFL-CIO reorganization in 2005, union membership saw a decline. In a 2009 study on low-wage workers in the nation's three largest cities, 26 percent suffered minimum wage violations, over 76 percent had worked over forty hours in the preceding week and had not been paid according to overtime laws, and some regions recorded noncompliance with the Fair Labor Standards Act (FLSA) at levels over 50 percent for work conducted in nursing homes, poultry processing plants, day care facilities, and restaurants.[29]

Burgeoning worker centers around the country increasingly played a role in helping workers make a case for fair treatment, making specific appeals for immigrant workers for whom existing unions are seldom an option.

Allegiance with national immigration reform campaigns is common across the majority of worker centers, which have strong ties to immigrant communities and are often led and staffed by migrant workers or leaders, such as Herrera, who grew up in that context. With most centers participating actively in immigration reform coalitions such as the National Council of La Raza, the National Immigration Forum, the National Network for Immigrant and Refugee Rights, the National Farmworker Justice Fund, and many others, the centers and their representatives have provided a significant vehicle for developing leadership and achieving important economic and political gains.[30]

Today, the COWC's website states that their work was inspired by *Wage Theft in America*, a 2008 book by Kim Bobo, who founded Interfaith Worker Justice. The website also states that the center had been conceived by a group of friends and allies who were united by a common vision for worker justice that culminated in the formation of the COWC. It received 501(c)(3) status in September of 2014. Even though Herrera and Pasquarello were not named on the site in 2022, the center's inception was indeed the result of much hard, unpaid work by a queer, Latinx man and his partner. Getting the COWC up and running had been the singular focus of Herrera and Pasquarello during their first years together, and ignoring this fact runs the risk of amplifying the myth of White, heterosexual saviorism.

To this point, I contacted Michael Smalz, a founding board member of the COWC and a cochair of their Worker Justice Committee. He confirmed that Herrera and Pasquarello had been there at the beginning, along with a small group of migrant rights activists and worker advocates and a handful of leaders of the local chapter of the Democratic Socialists of America that included Smalz, Connie Hammond, and Simone Morgen. Smalz also acknowledged that Herrera was the COWC's unpaid board president and chief spokesperson during the first several years of their existence.

In 2014, there had been only one other worker center in Ohio: the Cincinnati Interfaith Worker Center. The COWC's founders sought their advice and assistance, and they also communicated with the (now-defunct) national Interfaith Worker Center Association in Chicago. The interfaith organization in Chicago had received funding through the Catholic Diocese, which was not the model that Herrera and Pasquarello felt would have promoted intersectionality in the way they had envisioned. Instead, they drew inspiration from Dignidad Obrera in Nashville, Tennessee, which was active in a broad range of campaigns, had robust membership, was committed to intersectionality in the causes they championed, and was substantially self-funded through donations that allowed them to maintain a level of autonomy in their work.

Two events drove the founding of the COWC. The first was when Herrera, Pasquarello, and a small group of kindred spirits organized and held a May Day action in May of 2014. The second was the momentum they felt following their organizing work for the Coalition of Immokalee Workers (CIW).

Before 2014, there had not been a group that was making note of May Day in Columbus. They decided to call an action/protest for May Day of that year. Held in the downtown area, it was more celebratory in nature than an outright protest, but it was a powerful statement for people to gather to recognize and celebrate the workers of the world. The COWC went on to utilize May Day as a call to action in an intersectional manner beyond worker campaigns. As an example, in 2015, May Day took place shortly after Freddie Gray was murdered by Baltimore Police. The attendees incorporated "I am Freddie" signs to protest Gray's murder and endorsed Black Lives Matter as part of their May Day action. This is just one of many examples of how the two early founders envisioned the COWC: to be explicitly and unapologetically intersectional, with ample room to support BLM or take a public stance on Palestine.

In addition to May Day, the CIW campaigns were instrumental to the creation of the COWC. In 2014, Herrera and Pasquarello helped organize at the beginning of the Wendy's campaign, culminating in an eight-hundred-person march to Wendy's corporate headquarters in Dublin, Ohio. The two took positions in the CIW as full-time organizers at the time when the CIW shifted to the Wendy's campaign, which necessitated the local, on-the-ground support of experienced organizers. Having been one of the cofounders of the OSU Student/Farm Worker chapter, Pasquarello was heavily involved in student organizing, which was how Herrera and Pasquarello made their way into my classroom on that cold day in February. Herrera, for his part, was particularly adept at firing up the faith community and using a faith-informed vocabulary to bring people into the Fair Food campaign.

Heavily involved with the CIW and the Wendy's campaign from about 2014 to 2016, the idea for COWC taking root at that time was not a coincidence. The two were learning a lot from the CIW, which itself is classified as a highly successful worker center. Wanting to build off that momentum and the success of their May Day event, they hoped to harness the energy into something both local and durable. As such, COWC's support of "Boot the Braid," the campaign to boycott Wendy's until they signed on to the Fair Food campaign, was one of the issues that they aligned with and actively supported, and it became part of the organization's initial identity.

The group originally met in a series of spaces that were friendly to their cause, usually a private home or an office space Herrera happened to have at that time.

"Office space with Rubén was always a trip," Pasquarello said. "He had this ability to find free office space and operated like a nomad." Early on, the COWC worked out of an office at America Votes, a nonprofit that lent Herrera the space for free in the Short North area. But when America Votes had to move out, so did they.

After America Votes, they moved to a space at Summit on 16th United Methodist Church, which proved integral to their heavy involvement with the CIW and the Wendy's campaign. The Summit church was a solid supporter of the CIW, allowing them to set up shop in their offices several times. It eventually became an early headquarters for the COWC as well.

In the beginning, Spanish-speaking Ohioans would contact the organization because they knew Herrera was involved, and the COWC provided aid however they could manage. On one occasion, a woman called who desperately needed groceries when her husband was detained. On another occasion, a Spanish-speaking Columbus resident was missing several paychecks. He had been instructed to go to a particular Chase bank branch to collect his pay, which was to be provided in the form of debit cards. The bank's staff twice told him they didn't have his pay and there was nothing they could do. However, after Herrera and Pasquarello went with him to the same Chase location, they looked again and managed to find his pay.

"The power of showing up with advocates, confidence, and in a blazer, I swear," said Pasquarello, recalling the incident.

As the organization grew and began to draw the kind of funding that would eventually allow them to begin to pay staff, Pasquarello, who had been working as the volunteer treasurer, expressed the need for COWC to replace him in that role. He specifically pointed out that there was a conflict of interest: the treasurer and board president should not be living together. When he voiced this apprehension to COWC's newer leadership, he felt that his concern was dismissed. Sure enough, conflicts arose. After Herrera and Pasquarello left the COWC, they received complaints about how COWC had been footing the bill for Herrera's "personal" phone—the same phone that was publicly listed as the COWC phone line.

As noted, Herrera had been performing work for no pay for the first several years of COWC's operation. In the five-year period between completing his undergraduate degree and beginning law school at the Ohio

State University Moritz School of Law, Pasquarello worked many different jobs to foot the bills for their household. Many of his paychecks came from the education and nonprofit sectors, such as the Children's Defense Fund (CDF) Freedom Schools program, which provides summer and after-school enrichment; the Ohio Organizing Collaborative, where he created online and social media content; and the now-defunct Pomegranate Health Systems. In food services, he turned his high school experience working at Wawa ("objectively better than Sheetz") into gainful employment at the Torpedo Room restaurant at the Gateway Film Center, Brassica, and Third and Hollywood. Working as a cook, particularly once he started law school, provided a satisfying balance to the mental overload of problem-solving, reading, and endless exams. But more to the point of how he and Herrera managed their lives, Pasquarello was continually taking on jobs to pay for their groceries, rent, transportation, and other needs.

Eventually, the COWC Board managed to provide Herrera with a $500 a month stipend for the last six months or so of his service, and Pasquarello estimates that between the two of them, they had received approximately $3,000 for their three years of work. Obviously, they had not launched the COWC to hunt for fortune or fame. They did this because it mattered to them. But in the process, Pasquarello committed his own wages to help Herrera build the center ("the Pasquarello Foundation," he quipped), while Herrera, a man already in his midlife, worked full-time not only without pay but also without health insurance, retirement plans, or a net of savings underneath him. And if Pasquarello proposed Herrera get a checkup, the idea was promptly rejected—a no-fly zone in the relationship. Herrera's struggle for worker and migrant justice was done under great financial precarity. He was not making a living wage, but he labored tirelessly to ensure that others were.

Shortly after they left, the COWC developed more formal ties with organized labor and a more stable grant structure, and they eventually managed to provide compensation for their staff. At this time, the COWC has a paid outreach coordinator, whose position was made possible by a grant from the Franklin County Commissioners. The group is also preparing to hire a paid, full-time director in addition to another full-time staff person.

Today, the COWC is located at 2800 South High Street, and the mutual aid, or the more familial model of voluntary and reciprocal exchanges of resources and services that had been Herrera's modus operandi, eventually gave way to a membership organizational style. Current membership dues are fifteen dollars for low-income individuals and thirty-five dollars for others, and the group has stronger ties to local labor unions and federations than they had during its first years of operation.[31]

A testament to their success, the center has had many victories of note. They helped to draft and bring about the passage of the City of Columbus's landmark wage-theft ordinance in 2020.[32] Since 2013, they have continually prepared and distributed information on wage-theft laws and remedies and workers' rights and opportunities through videos, webinars, literature, websites, and in-person presentations. They assist workers in filing complaints, conduct investigations and refer wage-theft cases to their network of private attorneys, legal aid programs, and other worker centers that offer additional resources. They have strong ties to the Cincinnati Interfaith Worker Center and the Columbus Wage Theft Prevention and Enforcement Commission, and they provide mentorship to newer worker centers such as the Northeast Ohio Worker Center in Cleveland. While they are not a union, they lend support to workers who want to organize unions or protest poor pay and working conditions at their worksites.

For Pasquarello, these gains meant that the humble worker center that had been the focus of his first years together with Herrera grew to become an enduring part of Columbus's front line in the struggle for workers' rights. A significant moment that epitomizes Herrera's resistance and resilience, I submit that the COWC began as a true Columbus story: queer, centrifugal, and frequently playing out on the stage of pinche High Street.

Chapter V

TRUST THE CIRCLE

> It is possible the next Buddha will not take the form of an individual. The next Buddha may take the form of a community, a community practicing understanding and lovingkindness, a community practicing mindful living. And the practice can be carried out as a group, as a city, as a nation.
>
> —Thich Nhat Hanh

Occupying at least 90 percent of human history, the ancient hominins—our immediate ancestors—hunted, gathered, and camped. They used fire to warm themselves, cook food, and engineer the lived environment, and they gathered in community around the glow of its flames. Engagement with fire shifted human interactions in a process that, if we think about it, continues to unfold today among modern *Homo sapiens*, as the people of the planet figure out how to replace our fossil fuel combustion habits with more sustainable alternatives.

Wherever humans have gone in the world, they have carried with them language and fire.

Bringing people together for shared meals, safety, illumination, and conversation, our relationship with fire paved the way for the development of human community. Additionally, evidence about archaic humans has led many to conclude that meat cooked by fire provided more calories, potentially playing a pivotal role in the development of our larger brain size. The ability to cook food, the intellectual advantages this produced, and the new ways of organizing socially around meals prepared by fire are all fundamental to what it means to be human.

Humanity's control of fire is also thought to be important to the advancement of language, as gatherings around fire's life-giving glow required the development of speech forms that kept pace with a new matrix of listening and speaking to organize experience. The light, warmth, and safety that fire offered meant more activities could occur at night, contributing to prolonged verbal exchanges among kin and clan. This way of leaning toward the flames and seeing each other's gathered faces produced our ancestral social configuration: the instinctual shape around the fire's light and the heat it produced was the circle.[1]

A Different Elephant Story

One of the questions I posed to Herrera's close family and friends was about what he might have considered to be his greatest success in life.

"I think one success would be finishing school. Two, his success with Trust the Circle. The whole ideology behind it," Sanchez Murphy told me.

Herrera had begun to implement circle practice in Oregon, where he first incorporated the use of rocks as talking pieces to the Thanksgiving table. The communication approach helped break through scenarios in which everyone was talking at once on an issue, with some voices taking up more space than others. Sanchez Murphy saw him emphasize the circle because it brought silence and thoughtful introductions to a given gathering. "It was an occasion to learn more about the issue," she said, "listen to each other, and learn about each other's stories."[2]

"We were the first circle," Herrera's eldest daughter, Rita, recalled. After moving to Ohio, the family held regular meetings where they would sit down together and hold structured conversations to check in. She didn't remember using a talking piece but recalled that they were instructed to listen deeply without giving in to the temptation to silently rehearse what they would say when it was their own turn, as this would take away from their appreciation of what others were sharing. Rita estimated that their circles began when the older two children were in middle school and Naomi was preschool-age. These family gatherings took place at least once a month but were sometimes more frequent when there were larger issues that Herrera wanted to discuss.

Instead of a rigid organization around specific topics or goals, the gatherings offered a chance for family members to speak their minds. If a punishment was being doled out, they might discuss why the rule that had been broken was important, but more frequently, it was a space for simply listening to each other's feelings about what has happening in their lives at the time.

"What kind of things came up?" I asked over the course of our Zoom conversation.

"I think a lot of times jokes," said Rita. "He would ask us, 'Have you guys heard any new jokes?'"

"Do you remember a joke?"

Here, Rita hesitated. "Well, I mean, they were always kind of inappropriate," she said. I eventually convinced her to divulge and immediately understood why she had been inclined to hold back.

> My brother Ruben would tell the most. . . . One was about an elephant and a mouse on an island. And every night that mouse would go behind the elephant and have sex with it. One day

they were doing it and a coconut fell on the elephant's head. The elephant screamed, and the mouse said, "Suffer, bitch!"

When Rita shared this family moment with me, the first thing that came to mind was: What is it with the Herreras and their elephant stories? The second thing, though, was: How did their father react?

"When Ruben told the joke, my dad was like, 'Oh, my God.' . . . That's definitely a 'hashtag goals' moment of maturity when you think, 'Yeah, I'm gonna go ahead and go for that.'"

I'd like to point out here that this should not be interpreted as Herrera joking about sexual violence with his children. He had no idea what his son had been planning to say. Instead, the moment is included here as a testament to the way the two eldest children tested their father's boundaries and felt at ease disrupting the circle's solemnity with adolescent irreverence.

The story also has a fantastic denouement: "But the funniest part about that," continued Rita, "is that the next time we went to church . . . the pastor said, 'Have you ever heard the story about the elephant and the mouse?' We all froze and looked at each other. . . . I remember later on after church we were laughing so hard at that. We were having a panic attack."

"What was the pastor's version?"

"I don't even remember honestly. But it was something Biblical."

At first blush, the idea of a circle may seem too mundane or conventional to merit the emphasis that this book places on Herrera's cultivation of the shape as a container for important conversations. After all, many who were educated in the United States hold memories of their preschool or kindergarten circle in which a group of wiggling children were lulled into attention by a teacher's story or the chance to sing a favorite song together as a group. Because my first three years of school took place in the socially progressive environment of Eagle Rock Montessori School in Northeast LA, circle gatherings or similar activities had been a routine part of our day, a time in which the different voices of young people were taken into account by teachers who seemed to really value our input. It felt like being small did not preclude us from being important members of the community.

However, my educational experience shifted drastically when my brother and I next attended the day school associated with the Eagle Rock Baptist Church, which was located only a few blocks away from the Montessori school grounds. Our devoutly Catholic grandmother convinced our mother that we would receive a better education there than at our neighborhood's public school, and she said that its students were shining examples of what academically enriched and well-behaved young people should be.

My first weeks of third grade at our new Christian school were a shock. Instead of gathering in a circle on the floor, we were instructed to sit upright at our desks in silence, our hands crossed on top of the desk, our gaze continually directed toward the teacher rather than at each other. I recall thinking that it must have been a temporary drill or exercise that would soon give way to a more natural way of arranging ourselves, but no. This was to be our shape throughout the day. Students were conceived as passive, empty vessels rather than active participants in their own education.

I remember how terrifying it was to use the bathroom under this new regime. Instead of discretely letting a teacher know I needed to use the restroom in a room populated by different groupings of chattering students engaged in their own activities, I now had to wait for an opportune moment to raise my hand in front of everyone and ask for permission to use the bathroom pass. If we needed the pass more than twice during a given period of time, we would be punished by having our time at recess reduced. Once, I experienced the horror of needing to go a third time. Instead of succumbing to humiliation and punishment, I asked the teacher if I could get my jacket from the back of the class. She assented with a stern nod. I retrieved the jacket from my backpack, bunched it up tightly, and carefully positioned it underneath my skirt. I then peed on it in the classroom, which was a risk I preferred facing to the prospect of a third trip to the bathroom that would have been met with a reprimand and jeers. I managed to hide my soiled jacket from the teacher and my classmates, but it was a terrifying experience.

The point of the pyramidal, or vertical, model was clear. We children were not full human beings but rather incomplete and deficient adults. I longed for the ease of the circle and the feeling that my voice mattered. I eventually chalked the experience up to the pain of maturity, and I came to accept that the arrangement of students' bodies to maximize obedience and discipline was somehow more pleasing to God. I even harbored some suspicion that the relaxed and open model of engaging with students from my previous school might have been somehow sinful.

I offer this memory here to reflect on how welcoming young people into circle is no small thing, and it demonstrates how much intentional work Herrera put into creating a different family life for his children than the vertical and often abusive parenting he himself had received.

Circle practices of different stripes were broadly employed in the late nineties through the early aughts. Publications such as Jack Zimmerman and Virginia Coyle's *The Way of Council* (1996) and Christina Baldwin and Ann Linnea's *The Circle Way* (2010), among other titles, proliferated in the new millennium, and by the time these publications reached the general public, these types of practices had already been cropping up in schools, churches, leadership trainings, summer camps, and organizations where multivocal leadership was desired.

Thinking again of how Rita described the family's circle experience, one of the things her father had emphasized was that they should listen deeply and resist the temptation to be absorbed with preparing their own reply. This reminded me of the "listening from the heart" expression taken from Zimmerman and Coyle's "four intentions of council." The four intentions outlined in *The Way of Council* include "speaking from the heart," which entails an honest and nondefensive position; "listening from the heart," which means dedicating devout and attentive listening to the speaker; being "lean of expression," or finding brief and concise words to speak your truth; and finally, "spontaneity," which sets the intention to not mentally rehearse what was to be said.[3] From Sanchez Murphy and Rita's remarks about Herrera's use of the talking stick and how he explained the circle's intentions, it was clear that council practice had made its way to his spheres of activity in Oregon by the 1980s.

Also figuring prominently in the proliferation of circle practice was the Shambhala Institute's Authentic Leadership in Action (ALIA) summer program. Beginning in 2001 in Nova Scotia, ALIA, which hosts about 250 people a year, is described as a "vibrant meeting-place of people, practices, and ideas engaged at the frontier of organizational and societal change."[4]

In Columbus, the name that most often came up when I was trying to piece together the lineage of Herrera's circle practice was Phil Cass and the Art of Hosting approach. A leading figure in the growth of circle practice in Columbus, Cass holds a PhD in counseling and guidance from the Ohio State University and was the cofounder of the Physicians Leadership Academy, where he helped bring a mindfulness-based ethos of leadership to physicians of the Columbus Medical Association. Cass was inspired by the Art of Hosting (AoH) leadership style that he learned about in 2002 when he attended the ALIA program at the Shambhala Institute. There, he met dedicated practitioners of circle leadership from around the world who changed his entire approach to conflict resolution and the development of action plans.

Described as a set of social technologies that cultivate "order without control," the Art of Hosting is a set of core practices for how to host "conversations that matter": setting intention, creating hospitable space, asking powerful questions, surfacing collective intelligence, trusting emergence, finding mates, harvesting learning, and moving into wise action.[5] In the Art of Hosting method, the hero-style leader is supplanted by the listening-based leader who hosts conversations rather than dictates individual desires. Cass's efforts are credited with the significant redesign of Columbus's medical system leadership that began to incorporate the participatory methodologies he learned at Shambhala's ALIA workshop.

To learn more about the origins of Herrera's AoH involvement, I spoke with Rick Livingston. An Ohio resident and faculty member of the Ohio State University since 1993, Livingston first met Herrera at a four-day AoH training retreat around 2007 that was held at a Columbus Metro Park. A large-scale training, over sixty people from the government and nonprofit sectors were in attendance.

Livingston recounted that it had been Cass, along with his close friend Matt Habash, the executive director of the Mid-Ohio Foodbank and president of the Columbus City Council from 1999 to 2006, who led the charge on injecting the principles of the Art of Hosting into Columbus's civic infrastructure. Their goal was to bring enough people into the practice for it to become a common language for the city's leadership. At the training retreat, he found himself in the middle of many of the members of Columbus's civic leadership, who were getting together in the woods and revealing deeply held convictions and vulnerabilities to each other. "I'd read about all these people, and here they are," Livingston recounted.

When he met Herrera, it was immediately clear that he was not new to this kind of practice.

"Rubén was a soul," said Livingston. "He was able to embody things that, to me, spoke of deeper understanding. . . . I was a puppy. Rubén did not come off like a big dog. But he was definitely an older dog. He understood what was going on . . . there was definitely experience feeding into his participation in that network."[6]

Livingston's use of the word "soul" felt like a very apt description of Herrera. His Trust the Circle practice was akin to Quaker author Parker Palmer's "circle of trust" that he develops in *A Hidden Wholeness: The Journey toward an Undivided Life* (2004): "In a circle of trust, the powers of deformation are held at bay long enough for the soul to emerge and speak its truth. Here we are not required to conform ourselves to some external template. Instead, we are invited to conform our lives to the shape of our own souls." Comparing the soul to a wild animal, Parker writes, "Only by sitting quietly, breathing with the earth and merging with our surroundings, will the soul consider putting in an appearance."[7]

Livingston's remark that Herrera was a soul felt appropriate. He was someone who championed the discipline of welcoming, rather than chasing away, soulful things, and cultivating circles that provided the needed safety for the circles' participants to grow toward an authentic expression of the self.

Herrera incorporated AoH and similar practices in the circles he convened across family and activist networks throughout his organizing years in Columbus. Leticia Vazquez-Smith confirmed in our conversation about Herrera's leadership style that what Latinx community leaders looked forward to in their gatherings was his way of implementing circle dialogue, and his relationship to the AoH practice was even mentioned in the Baldwin and Linnea book.

In a section titled "Healing the Family Lineage," *The Circle Way* focuses on the call that Herrera put out on the Art of Hosting electronic mailing list in search of someone practicing this model in the Portland area. In 2008, the youngest Herrera sister, Ruth Marie, was dying of breast cancer at the age of forty-eight. Herrera and Ruth Marie were the youngest of what had become a family of nineteen grandchildren and a dozen great-grandchildren spread across several states. They had not been together since 1982, and both Ruth Marie and Herrera felt as though they were reliving the experience of their mother's cancer that had occasioned the initial fracturing of their family. Ruth Marie resolved that she would turn the tragedy of her illness into the triumph of bringing the family together again.

The family understood this gathering to be her last big wish. The hosting (facilitator) role was taken up by Steve Ryman, the AoH practitioner who answered Herrera's call for an Oregon-based host so that Herrera could participate in the circle along with the rest of his family.

Not everyone was comfortable with the idea. Around thirty-five family members attended, but a few of the older brothers were resistant.

They arrived late, and there had been grumblings about how it wasn't appropriate for Ruth Marie and Herrera—the youngest siblings—to assume a position of leadership in the family. One of the older brothers arrived after the three-hour circle was already halfway over. Ryman felt the awkwardness at times when newcomers had to be incorporated into the circle, but they pressed on, working to maintain the deeper level of conversation that they had already reached and to pull the patriarchs into deeper honesty.

> One thing that touched my heart was watching the men struggle with their emotions. Several profound apologies were made. Another late-arriving brother no one had seen for years. I don't know if they even knew he was coming. He talked about how far away he'd grown from the family and how much he wanted something different.[8]

Working through the moments of volatility, the collective experience helped ground the Herreras in their shared experience and produce a shift of consciousness. The circle practice provided the opportunity to share how much they continued to mean to each other.

I reached out to Ryman in 2020 to ask him about the experience.

"I have to say," I told him, "I can't imagine a circle that is called by somebody in the advanced stages of a cancer diagnosis the way Ruth Marie did."

"My recollection of it," said Ryman, "was that I was a much younger and less experienced practitioner at that time, and I was scared shitless. This was a very challenging invitation and one that I welcomed, but, as I recall, there were probably fifteen people in the circle, all of Rubén's siblings were there, and many with their spouses. . . . It was multigenerational and I remember Rubén's desire to call this circle and his desire to be a participant in it. . . . And it was one of the most incredible circles I'd ever been a part of. I'm very grateful."[9]

Calling the circle had been a gesture Herrera and Ruth Marie made in order to foster emotional healing and spiritual alignment in their family lives. In the book, Herrera states:

> We knew we had had a mother who loved us in those early years and we couldn't remember her. And those who could remember her never talked about her. So we did what we could to recapture that period in our family life. When I went to Texas, I asked people, "Tell me stories of my mother, tell me stories of my father, tell me about your relationship with them and with us." I took the common things from all these interviews to Ruth Marie, and we pieced our lives together.[10]

Ruth Marie passed away in April of 2009, surrounded by Herrera and other family members. The gathered siblings spoke with her in soft voices, sharing love and embodying the peace that they had sought and won.

The siblings also found themselves speaking to their mother, Pura Castilla, through Ruth Marie. They told their mother things at Ruth Marie's bedside that they never had the chance to tell her while she was living, and they collectively brought the comfort to their youngest sister and to each other that had been stolen when they were young. Ruth Marie spoke her last words to Herrera over the phone before he boarded the plane in Ohio to be with her in Oregon.

"Remember the circle."

The Columbus Model, Part Two

At a certain moment in my conversation with Ryman, he casually referred to Columbus, Ohio, as the "mecca" of the Art of Hosting practice.

Aside from college football, it's unusual to think of Columbus as the mecca—or spiritual center—of anything. Take, for example, the good-natured ribbing that Tom and Ray Magliozzi would spin on their radio show, *Car Talk*, which was broadcast weekly on National Public Radio stations for many years. With their working-class Boston accents and boisterous laughter, the two brothers would revel in wisecracks at the expense of anything and everything their caller discussed. Shortly after moving to Ohio, I listened as a caller phoned in to discuss a car problem. When the caller identified themselves as a Columbus resident, the brothers immediately began to riff on the city, triumphantly christening it with a new nickname: "Gateway to Toledo!"

True, the city suffers from a dearth of promising epithets. Obviously, it's unhappy official name comes from the foundational myth of European colonization. In Spanish, Columbus's name is Cristóbal Colón, and the last name coincides with the first part of the word "colonizer": "colonizador." The Latin word is prettier: Columbus means "dove," from the Italian "colombo." (Something was lost in translation, since the Spanish word for dove is "paloma.") Recent nicknames for the city have included "Discovery City," "Arch City," "Cap City," and "Cbus." The *New York Times* has gone as far to report on the city's lack of identity. As Erik Eckholm's 2010 article titled "There May Be 'No Better Place,' but There Is a Better Slogan" describes it:

> This capital city in the middle of a state better known, fairly or not, for cornfields and rusting factories has a low cost of living, easy traffic and a comparatively robust economy. It variously has been pronounced to have the nation's best zoo, best science museum and best public library. For sports fans, "Ohio State Buckeyes" says it all. What Columbus does not have, to the despair of its leaders, is an image.[11]

As you can see, Columbus's lack of discernable identity is a dilemma that plays out on the national stage. Without a consistent core message that different groups embrace, a Midwest city that can boast both one of the country's largest state fairs (hello, butter sculpture!) and one of the largest LGBTQ+ Pride parades (hello, Mennonite float!) is the kind of place that, when Steve Ryman of Oregon calls it a mecca, you are surprised.

"Columbus," continued Ryman, "is the poster child for Art of Hosting in the whole world."

How is that possible?

Ryman explained the origin story, noted above, concerning Phil Cass and the Shambhala Center, and how the scale with which the trainings were offered and implemented led to hundreds of people receiving training in the AoH approach. Thanks to professional ties and the outreach efforts of its early pioneers, this leadership model made its way not only into the medical system (Cass) and the food bank system (Habash) but also into parts of the community, where Herrera brought his own background to the practice and shared it broadly in various activity spheres around the city.

Officially called "Art of Hosting and Harvesting Conversations that Matter," AoH websites, published literature, and conversations with practitioners describe a practice that draws on various conversational methodologies, including World Café, Open Space, and appreciative inquiry, to form the core of their two three-day intensive trainings.

The first thing I noticed is that the "fourfold" Art of Hosting structure was similar to the "four intentions" of council practice described in *The Way of Council*. One: Be Present (come undistracted and clear about the need for the conversation and what your personal participation can be). Two: Participate and practice conversations (listening carefully and without judgments). Three: Host conversations (take responsibility for creating and holding the space for a group of people). Four: Co-create (show up for a conversation and contribute).[12]

And what might this look like in a practical sense?

For Ryman, the basic circle practice begins by welcoming people and framing the circle's purpose and intention. The conversation begins with checking in, but what happens from there depends on the gathering's purpose. Based on the circle's intention, there will be a question or sometimes a series of questions that everybody in the circle has the opportunity to respond to. At the end, there is a checkout, which is a way of bringing closure to the experience.

"How would you suggest the layperson get involved in this kind of practice?" I asked.

"One of the sayings we have in the art of hosting is never host alone. . . . The role of the guardian is to attend to the energetic temperature of the group and to call the group back to the purpose that's in the center. To slow the process down when necessary to, to pause if necessary."

Typically, the host and the guardian sit across from each other, and the guardian provides assurance and eye contact to let the host know they are not in it alone. I also learned that it's important for someone new to the hosting practice to find someone to host with who has the benefit of more experience.

"Even if someone is not terribly experienced in hosting a circle, I think circles can still do so much," he added. "And the more one becomes skilled, there's something about inviting depth of experience within the circle that allows more to arise."

The question-driven AoH structure, along with some of the organization's prompts from the training described by Livingston ("What time is it in Columbus?") made their way into Herrera's approach to the circle. Herrera was also inclined to write Facebook posts that consisted of a series of questions, such as the following list he posted on April 1, 2019:

—How will I live through this change?
—How do I take care of myself? My loved ones? Of strangers? Of my neighbor?
—And who is my neighbor?
—From what sources do I draw my values, my strength?
—What has meaning?
—Where are my borderlands?

—Who am I?
—Why am I here?

The series of open-ended questions, posted in a public place, were a call to contemplation. Rather than using social media as a space for angry rants, Herrera's Facebook community was invited to consider their own thoughts about these issues in a horizontal, rather than vertical, arrangement. As a queer, BIPOC elder in Ohio, he mixed and took from his previous council practice experience and his Columbus-based AoH trainings to connect individuals and communities to provide a container in which compassion and empathetic listening could thrive.

This is not to say that Herrera was wholly uncritical of this work.

As I've noted before, Herrera very fervently resisted conventional forms. As soon as something became stable, fixed, or regimented, he was already interrogating its maxims and moving toward the next challenge, both in his faith and as an agent for social change. A Facebook post from October 18, 2018, simply reads: "Art of Hosting Conversations vs. Art of Doing." If ten years prior he had sought an AoH practitioner to provide the scaffolding for Ruth Marie's call for a family reunion, he was also comfortable challenging the notion that hosting "conversations that matter" was the goal in and of itself.

I asked Livingston what he made of the potential division between coming together in a circle and taking collective action, and I found his answer to be helpful: "I recognize [how] an aspect of the discourse of the American Left is impatience with dialogue, and that seems to be . . . a truncated conception of what action is. Like, 'If action doesn't happen *tomorrow*, it's just talk.'"

Livingston's reflection on the "truncated idea" of how well-meaning progressives define action made me think of Herrera's choice to name one of his central focus groups the "Ohio *Action* Circle." Yes, they were coming together to hold conversations that mattered, but they were doing so with the common goal of catalyzing change. Without inclusive and equitable dialogue, any resulting actions would have risen out of the hero-based model that Herrera was intent on undermining. And, as chapter 3 pointed out, the geographic dispersion of Latinx communities throughout the city meant that a centering practice was key to creating a sense of belonging, mutual visibility, and enfranchisement in a city with scant public spaces designed to acknowledge, promote, and celebrate Latinidad. Trust the Circle was the name he gave to this convergence of needs and opportunities that was specific to Columbus.

Círculo y espíritu

Above, I've discussed the extremely important contributions of Zimmerman and Coyle, Baldwin and Linnea, and Cass and Habash, who have each amplified the prospects of circle practice at the international, national, and local levels. However, this does not mean that the practice is exclusive to White, Western spaces of community building. In Herrera's case, one of the tributaries that resulted in his engagement with Trust the Circle practice included his spiritual embodiment of mestizaje, or the mixture of ancestral Mesoamerican Indigenous and Spanish ancestry.

In *The Way of Council*, Zimmerman and Coyle begin with an anecdote about the experience of a Pueblo Native American who was introduced to the practice of tribal council for the first time. There, he witnessed the use of a talking stick and the process by which his grandfather's Pueblo community arrived at a decision in the depth of silence. The authors attribute their version of council practice to such Native American councils of elders, as well as to Quaker meetings, and note that the talking stick is rooted in Indigenous ceremony.

Originally called a "speaker's staff," the talking stick (or any other centering object—Herrera had used rocks in Oregon) is used by many Native American nations. Zimmerman and Coyle write, "In implementing council in contemporary settings, we have shared the concern of many people, Native American and others, about the appropriation of one culture's sacred ceremonies by another. Our aim has always been to practice a form of council that honors the spirit of the ancient ceremonies without the pretense of being traditional." They conclude that many forms of council belong to all who gather in the circle to "embrace the challenge of listening and speaking from the heart."[13]

When I posed the question to Ryman about the problem of cultural appropriation in AoH practices, it didn't seem like it was the first time he had been asked something along these lines.

"It's my understanding," said Ryman, "that circle is the earliest human experience. The prehistoric people would come back after a day of hunting and sit around the fire and share stories. . . . In that context, it . . . makes Native Americans seem pretty modern."[14] However, he also acknowledged that not everyone felt the same.

> I've done a little bit of work in Australia where some members of the Aboriginal culture don't like to use a talking piece, because they say that is from the Native American culture, and it's appropriation of another culture. But within the Aboriginal culture, they have their own practices of sitting in circle, and it's a little bit different.

In his statements, Ryman joined with Baldwin and Linnea in asserting that the DNA of the practice goes back to early humans and was widely engaged across ancient cultures, while also understanding that the specific device of the talking piece was connected to the First Peoples of the US, rather than the European settler colonizers who came afterward. After all, the Indigenous Australians Ryman mentioned did not ascribe the talking piece to the Calvinists of New England or the Catholic mendicant orders of New Spain and Mexico that later became part of the Southwest. They saw it as Native American, pertaining to the Indigenous cultures of the United States. While the circle originated with the earliest humans, the way the practice is structured comes from unique cultural genealogies that are acknowledged in different ways.

For Herrera, Trust the Circle was the evolution of organizational shifts that arose over the years in his own activist experience, moving from the hero-based movements helmed by César Chávez and José Ángel Gutiérrez in Oregon into more open forms of shared leadership that he employed in his years as an Ohioan. While he was informed by AoH and other tributaries that shaped his approach, there was also a unique cultural genealogy behind Trust the Circle that should be considered as well.

As with the Tejano healing rituals that his paternal grandmother Julia implemented in their early childhood, curanderismo (Mexican folk healing) played a role in the Herrera family's spirituality. As described in the first chapter, when Herrera suffered persistent night terrors in the wake of his mother's death, a healing ritual to cure susto had been a helpful treatment.

Along with susto, several illnesses prevalent in the borderlands can trace their roots back to pan-Mesoamerican beliefs. Greater Mesoamerica—what I am calling the past and present Indigenous cultures associated with maize-based, pre-Hispanic societies and their descendants such as the Mexica (Aztec) and Maya—is the lineage Mexican Americans reference when they self-describe as Chicano or, in recent times, Chicanx, which Herrera certainly did. Mesoamerican ancestry, along with its conceptions of the body as intrinsically tied to communal—rather than individual—spiritual and physical wellness, is at the core of Chicanx, non-Western ideas of health.

For instance, the illness of envidia belongs to a family of illnesses variably ascribed either to witchcraft or to garden-variety ill will. It translates to English as "envy," but the spiritual implications of envidia in the Mesoamerican context imply a disease load that gets lost in translation. Envy and ambition—energies born of egotism and greed—are viewed as corruptions of the healthy person. The desire for communal, rather than individual, health and prosperity is seen to maintain equilibrium among the members of a community.[15]

Along with envidia, a medical complaint rooted in excessive individual desire is mal de ojo ("evil eye"), an illness produced by extreme admiration. The most common type of ojo in the Mexican and Chicanx settings is unwitting admiration for children's beauty and health. Babies are particularly prone to this illness—how can you help but admire an infant? Young children are often decorated with mal de ojo bracelets, charms that work against ojo.

Along with susto, belief in ojo was present in Herrera's family life into adulthood. At one point, when Rita was still a baby, Herrera was told that someone had afflicted her with ojo. They encircled a small charm bracelet around her wrist: it was intended as protection from the disease caused by excessive admiration, and an acknowledgement that individual distinction could leave someone susceptible to cosmic peril.

The system of compadrazgo, or godparent networks, are fundamental to the fabric of Greater Mesoamerica, as these constitute a way for the more well-off members of the community to redistribute resources to the less advantaged. As such, elaborate quinceañeras (a girl's fifteenth birthday celebration) and weddings held by families of modest economic means are possible: they are the result of a matrix of godparents who chip in to make large-scale events possible and create moments of communal revelry.

In order to understand more about the system of beliefs at the heart of Herrera's implementation of circle practice, I spoke with Herrera's youngest daughter, Marisa Garverick Herrera. A professional education consultant, it would be difficult to imagine a career more in keeping with both her parents' values than the work Marisa performs. "I always say that I'm a pretty good mix of my parents," she said. "My mom was a public school teacher for nearly forty years. And, of course, my father's work very much was centered around the needs of Black and Indigenous people of color and advancing equity."

Starting out as a kindergarten teacher teaching predominantly Mexican, first-generation students, Marisa moved from there into coaching and teaching about how to introduce more culturally responsive practices in educational settings. Working in school districts across the country, her father's circle practice was an important influence on her leadership style, which she sees as an aspect of shared Indigenous ancestry and an expression of a spiritual inheritance:

> The practice of circle . . . it comes from way before us, from folks who came from this land, some of which were our ancestors. To me, that's very important to acknowledge, especially in my professional life, and particularly when I'm working with educators. We know that educators, meaning teachers and school leaders—the people that are in front of our children teaching them—in America are predominantly White. So, I think that's a very important acknowledgement, just like it is important to acknowledge the land in which we occupy that belonged to Indigenous groups.[16]

In both Ryman's and Marisa's statements, they describe circle practice as something that is both ancient and sacred. Ryman is not wrong to take a wide anthropological view that locates the circle in the earliest human societies. And Marisa is not wrong in attributing the resurgence of the practice to Indigenous groups as a more recent model for the Western recuperation of this way of knowing. In her work, where she deals with predominantly White professionals in the education sector, who are frequently unaccustomed to imagining that powerful practices can come from Indigenous sources, she acknowledges this genealogy plays a role in actualizing the cultural visibility and inclusion that is her professional mission to foster.

For me, the non-Western qualities of Herrera's approach to circle, and what his community members are getting at when they employ Trust the Circle as a shorthand for his ethos as an activist and catalyst, was the centrifugal force that was consistent with Mesoamerican healing, whereby excessive ego was equated with pathology, and the consistent redistribution of resources was associated with the alignment of physical and spiritual wellness. Instead of a patriarch at the top of the pyramid, the circle brings its participants together as equals to really see and hear each other, not only in a tradition with our ancient hominin foremothers and forefathers but also as a more recent network of compadres and camaradas who share concerns about the ills born of envy and greed and who come together to counter the excessive focus on the individual.

The most telling example of how Herrera understood the circle as a fusion of his cultural, spiritual, and activist beliefs comes from the Foulis interview. Upon asking him about the aspects of his Latino culture he worked to maintain as an Ohioan, he initially mentioned his nostalgia around traditions such as heritage food and music. But he concluded his response by talking about the act of listening as a cultural form of respect and blessing:

> Spirituality, people in the community who know me and have done some work with us, . . . they'll always bless me. "*Que dios te bendiga.*" . . . It's spiritual, but it's also a circle of respect. And I think that we can't lose that. . . . We get caught up by that which has bound us: Greed and money and material things, and [saying] "it's mine." . . . I'm human, I make mistakes as well. But how can I . . . [be] intentional about this, even if it's just sitting still and listening.[17]

Above, we can see that Herrera's circle was both culturally and spiritually charged. Listening with intention was his way of sharing blessing—the activation of a type of "counter spell" to protect its users from the forces of excessive greed and egotism. Listening was his way of telling people in his circle, Que Dios los bendiga.

The Columbus Sanctuary Collective / El Colectivo Santuario de Columbus

> Both Espinal and Vargas are mothers, and it is largely for their children that they have made such enormous sacrifices. #SanctuaryForAll #KeepEdithHome #LetMiriamStay
>
> —Rubén Castilla Herrera, Facebook Post, November 2, 2018

When Quasimodo rushes Esmeralda into the Notre Dame Cathedral crying "Sanctuary!" this literary figure, reinterpreted in live action and animated films alike in modern times, was actually participating in a concept that predates Christianity and goes back at least as far as the time when Roman and Greek temples offered protection to fugitives.[18] Early Christian churches, in part out of the need to compete with pagan temples, also extended their places of worship to people who were fleeing imprisonment or worse. Sanctuary within the confines of holy grounds meant that no one could come in and arrest, harm, or remove someone who had fallen on the wrong side of secular authority.

In recent decades in the United States, the sanctuary movement was both a religious and political campaign in response to federal immigration policies that targeted Central Americans fleeing violent civil conflict for deportation. At its peak in the 1980s, over five hundred congregations were involved in sanctuary efforts, providing physical refuge, resources, and often legal counsel to the refugees they harbored in churches belonging to a range of denominations that included, but was not limited to, Catholic, Lutheran, Methodist, Baptist, Jewish, Unitarian, Mennonite, and Quaker. These parishes derived their social teachings from the Civil War, the Underground Railroad, and the civil rights struggles of the 1960s, as well as the sanctuary provided to conscientious objectors escaping the Vietnam War draft in the 1970s.

Fast-forward to 2016, when Donald Trump was elected to the country's highest office, not in spite of his overtly racist sentiments toward immigrants and refugees but because of them. With his key campaign promise to "build a wall" on the US-Mexico border, Trump played on the rhetoric of "us" versus the "other," targeting immigrants and crying "fake news" whenever he was accused of holding White supremacist views. He was inaugurated in January of 2017, and by 2018, hate groups in the United States had risen to a record high of 1,012 after three years of steady decline under the Obama administration. "Observing Trump's rhetoric, one can understand how hate groups could feel emboldened," reported Dylan and Mather in *Political Science* in 2020.[19]

Following Herrera's involvement with CIW campaigns, I reconnected with him during the anti-hate rallies that were organized to protest Trump's virulent language and campaign pledges that dominated the national discourse from 2015 to 2016. Many photos from that year depict Herrera wearing a large poncho painted to resemble a brick wall emblazoned with the words "Wall Off Trump." In 2015, he recruited me to bring my "Miss Illegal Alien Ohio" performance art persona to an anti-hate rally in front of the Columbus Convention Center, where Trump was speaking. For my Miss Illegal Alien Ohio costume, I painted my face green, wore a silver lamé dress from the 1960s, and gave brief speeches in the style of a beauty pageant contestant, declaring that "Intergalactic beauty starts with us!" Obviously, Herrera and I were both okay with performing in unusual costumes to bring attention to the absurdity of the political moment.

In 2016, as the world reeled with the news of Trump's victory over Hillary Clinton, Herrera quickly sprang into action to join with Latinx Ohio's most vulnerable community members. When Herrera and Pasquarello traveled to Pasquarello's home state of Pennsylvania in December of 2017, the pair met with Carmela Apolonio Hernández and her four children. Her asylum appeal had just been denied, and she and her children were faced with deportation orders. The family took sanctuary at the Church of the Advocate, a Black Episcopalian church in

North Philadelphia with historical ties to civil rights activism.[20] Meeting with Hernandez's family and her attorney, David Bennion, Herrera—who was already involved in the sanctuary case of Edith Espinal as detailed below—discussed the kinds of grassroots strategies that were called for in that moment. Bennion would go on to tell Pasquarello that their visit in 2017 was the seed life of what came to be called the Colectivo Santuario. The group eventually spanned seven states—Colorado, Missouri, North Carolina, Ohio, Pennsylvania, Texas, and Virginia—and Herrera's unique talent for igniting action through conversation had been central to its emergence.

By 2018, the Colectivo Santuario served as a nationwide coalition that included immigrants in sanctuary, organizers, attorneys, and members of pro-migrant faith communities. The organization supported the difficult decision made by people who were facing impending deportation under the Trump administration to enter churches for sanctuary. While it was a safe place for people facing deportation, sanctuary was not a goal in and of itself: it meant strict confinement for indeterminate stretches of time.

The undocumented members of the collective who went into sanctuary were referred to as "sanctuary leaders," and over the course of their stay on church premises, they shared strategies and mutual support while seeking a legislative route for protections that would allow them to leave confinement but remain in the country. Colectivo members participated in weekly phone and video calls with each other. "They were using Zoom before it was cool," noted Pasquarello.[21]

Edith Espinal sought sanctuary at the Columbus Mennonite Church on October 2, 2017, in order to avoid being deported back to her native country of Mexico—a process that would have separated her from her three children and husband. Under the Trump administration, Espinal had been denied a stay of removal before she entered sanctuary because, as ICE officials informed her, she was an "enforcement priority."

Edith Espinal, Rubén Castilla Herrera, and Espinal's daughter, Stephanie Gonzalez, courtesy of photographer Stephen Pavey.

I first met Espinal at the home of Herrera and Pasquarello when they organized a summer evening get together for a representative of Mijente, an intersectional organization that was grounded in Latinx issues but was inclusive of campaigns for racial, economic, gender, and climate justice as well. Herrera was the city's link to Mijente's networks and resources, which had been formed in 2015 after the #Not1More Deportation campaign. This made sense: they were one of the most prominent organizations to counter the growing threats to the Latinx community, but they did this in a wholly intersectional way.

Edith Espinal and her husband, Manuel González, were present at that meeting, and, as was the modus operandi at a Herrera and Pasquarello gathering, all were welcome to introduce themselves and talk about the issues that mattered to them. I recall Espinal being a voice for undocumented Columbus residents and thinking that she was someone who, although soft-spoken, emanated an air of unmistakable strength and conviction.

After most of the attendees left, Espinal remained behind to speak to Herrera and the Mijente representative further about the threat of deportation and the prospect of going into sanctuary. That evening, they discussed the case of Elvira Arellano, a woman who had gained national recognition when she took sanctuary in a Chicago church in August 2006 to avoid being deported. Herrera pledged that if Espinal wanted to take this course of action, he would help her find a church that was suitable. They knew she could be deported at any time.

Certain conditions needed to be met before Espinal could seek and obtain sanctuary in Columbus. First, an Obama-era memo classified churches, hospitals, and schools as "sensitive locations," or places where immigration officials were not allowed to take enforcement actions. Second, the Columbus Mennonite Church, as a congregation, was willing to provide her with this type of support. An attorney spoke with the church's pastor, Joel Miller, and walked him through the legal implications, explaining that providing sanctuary could lead to a felony conviction and that he could be prosecuted for harboring her.

I met up with Rev. Miller on a warm day in October of 2022 to ask him about how the congregation came to the decision to become Ohio's first public sanctuary church of the Trump administration. While a nonpublic case in Northeast Ohio at a Unitarian Universalist church had preceded the Columbus Mennonite Church's action, Espinal had been the first to garner media attention and a political spotlight for seeking sanctuary.

"Did you understand that you were risking your own freedoms, and that you could be charged with a felony?" I asked.

"It was definitely raised," he replied.

On Thursday, August 24, 2017, Rev. Miller joined with members of the Faith in Public Life organization to meet with Herrera and Espinal and a small group of her advocates at a coffee shop on the West Side. While other church leaders were in attendance, none were able to offer a place for Espinal to stay. It was announced that Espinal had exhausted all her options and needed to take action immediately. An emergency meeting of the Mennonite church's leadership team was convened on August 26. They then presented Espinal's need for sanctuary to the congregation during the following day's service, where it was agreed upon that they would, and should, offer the premises for sanctuary.[22]

"We knew that we were in a kind of unprecedented times with Trump doing unprecedented things, but it did help that from the eighties movement, even when there were some . . . convictions . . . people never served jail time or never had to pay fees," Rev. Miller said.[23] The congregation needed to take this history into account before making such a consequential decision.

Rev. Miller noted that Herrera was crucial in bringing the city's interfaith leaders around to the sanctuary cause. When he put out a request for assistance to find a suitable sanctuary space for Espinal amongst a cadre of faith-based leaders in Columbus, his language did not rest on unfair policies, human rights, critical race theories, or the concept of immigration reform under the Trump administration. The message was, "Edith needs our help," which helped bring home the stakes of their commitment and the urgency of meeting the call.

Congregants were united in accepting the risk to house Espinal, and a blog entry dated from October of 2017 explained: "When Mennonites tell our history we remember a time when we too sought sanctuary from violence, and came to places like this country. Now we are in a position to offer sanctuary. Our decision was grounded in this memory, along with one of the most basic teachings of any faith: 'Love thy neighbor.'"[24]

The third factor contributing to Espinal's ability to take sanctuary in Columbus was the ordinance the city council had passed in June of 2017 to protect immigrants in sanctuary. Ordinance 1304-2017 prohibits "denial of city services, misuse of city resources, and solicitation of information about a person's immigration status by City employees or officials."[25] Sponsored by Zach M. Klein, the ordinance was inspired by a meeting city council member Elizabeth Brown had with Espinal and other immigrants to provide protections from aggressive immigration enforcement.

Since there is no official legal definition of what a "sanctuary city" is, the meaning of this term varies greatly from place to place. In general terms, the local law enforcement in a sanctuary jurisdiction will refuse to cooperate with federal immigration authorities to arrest undocumented migrants who are stopped and apprehended for minor offenses. In many cases, the sanctuary jurisdiction would oppose laws like those proposed by Arizona's SB 1070 that would require state law enforcement officers to determine an individual's immigration status, and Georgia's HB 87, which made the transportation of undocumented immigrants a crime punishable by steep fines and a prison sentence of up to a year.[26] That Columbus officials were willing to get behind this executive order made it clear that local police were not to be in the business of enforcing federal immigration laws. It was a heartening step in the right direction, and it was the result of the steady pressure that Herrera and the organizations he worked with had been applying.

After Espinal, the Colectivo Santuario soon included another member. In June of 2018, a Honduran woman named Miriam Vargas entered sanctuary at the First English Lutheran Church on Columbus's Near East Side. Entering the US in 2005, Vargas sought to escape violence and lack of employment opportunities in her country of origin. Married and with two daughters in the States, she saw her residency in the US as a way to ensure greater safety and more opportunities for her family.

When ICE showed up at Vargas's door in 2013, she feared a deportation order. Instead, she was ordered to check in with ICE every six months for five years. However, similar to Espinal's case, the deportation order eventually arrived, and people like her, undocumented residents with no criminal offenses, were hit hard by the Trump administration's policy of zero tolerance for undocumented residents. Herrera took Vargas to meet Espinal, who spoke to her about her experience in sanctuary at the Mennonite Church.

"She told me how difficult it is to live in sanctuary," Vargas said. "But she told me, 'You can do it. Don't be separated from your family. Your voice has validity. And Rubén is going to help us. He's going to lift our voices.' And he has."[27]

Miriam Vargas and Herrera, November 20, 2018, courtesy of photographer Maddie McGarvey.

It was in the context of a Colectivo Santuario event for Miriam Vargas that my penchant for absurdity and Chicanx humor again intersected with a cause that Herrera championed. The event was a quesadilla dinner fundraiser, and I waited with Moriah Flagler—a friend and civic theatre collaborator—in a long line to receive our eagerly anticipated plate. Instead of feeling sullen about the wait, I was in high spirits. It felt like it was the right place to be, which was a feeling I always had when I saw Herrera and Pasquarello darting about, greeting people, and rallying spirits. I had recently finished my book *Food Fight! Millennial Mestizaje Meets the Culinary Marketplace* (2019), and my thoughts were continually churning through ways in which food could be harnessed as a force for good, such as the fundraiser where we found ourselves.

Quesadillas, but make it justice.

As a politically engaged performance artist and poet, I wanted a way to connect the dots for people between the nation's inexhaustible appetite for Latin American foods and the national rejection of Latin American people. I suddenly found myself in a grin-infused conversation with Herrera about the city's need for a "Taco Reparations Brigade." While the language for the title of this "brigade" came to me while waiting in line for my quesadilla, it was steeped in a legacy of Chicanx movement humor, taking a page from the Royal Chicano Air Force (RCAF), a seminal California-based art collective founded in 1970 by Ricardo Favela, José Montoya, and Esteban Villa. Again, reflecting on the way that Herrera had immediately imparted a sense of Chicanx community and belonging to my life in Ohio, that was a moment when my Chicana-based parlance surfaced because I knew it had a ready recipient. Herrera would get it.

From that initial moment of reveling in the flippancy of Chicanx-style resistance and agreeing on the need for a Taco Reparations Brigade, very soon after the quesadilla fundraiser, that was what we became. With Herrera, Pasquarello, and artists Laura "LROD" Rodriguez, Bryan Ortiz, and Moriah Flagler, we developed an action that would use Mexican lucha libre wrestling motifs and the distribution of our MenuFesto pamphlet to create awareness about defamatory messages in White-owned Columbus taco shops and the juxtaposition of cultural appropriation and increased deportations. The Taco Reparations Brigade has performed several lucha-themed actions as well as processional performances around the Day of the Dead in Columbus since our initial action that took place in front of a Condado restaurant in 2018. I eventually edited elements of the original pamphlet's language into my "MenuFesto" poem that I include in the "Hasta la Victoria Mix Tape" section at the end of the book.

On February 25, 2019, about two years after Columbus's Mayor Ginther signed Ordinance 1304-2017 into law, the Columbus City Council passed a resolution to keep immigrant families together. Although the resolution didn't change any policies or make it possible for Espinal and Vargas to leave the confines of their respective Columbus churches, it was a significant show of support. The resolution made it clear to Homeland Security that there was strength in numbers behind the sanctuary movement in Ohio, making it politically expensive for ICE to move forward on their deportation orders involving Espinal and Vargas.[28]

The resolution represented a victory for the Colectivo Santuario, but when I spoke with Espinal, she didn't discuss the ordinance or the resolution as the key factors that helped her remain with her family. Instead, it was Herrera's efforts that she saw as being the heart of her struggle and source of strength: "Él siempre fue. En la tarde se iba a su casa, me llamaba, me mandaba mensaje. Para mí fue 24 horas," Espinal told me when I met with her at her home on the West Side. ("He was always there. In the afternoon he would go back to his house where he called me, he'd send me messages. He was there for me twenty-four hours a day.")[29]

"How did Herrera help you? What had been his main contribution?" I asked her. In response, she heaved a sigh that conveyed how difficult it would be to sum up what he had done for her. "I learned from him how to fight, and how to have the courage to do it," she told me. She added that he taught her the importance of coming out of the shadows:

> La importancia de enseñarnos a que tenemos que luchar a salir de las sombras. De no tener miedo a luchar. Siempre estaba dispuesto a luchar por los demás. Siempre estaba dispuesto a ayudar a la comunidad. Creo que eso fue lo que él nos enseñó. Hay que luchar sin miedo y hay que salir por delante.[30]

After Vargas went into sanctuary, Herrera's time had to be divided between the two churches as he rushed to help connect the new sanctuary leader with the resources she and her children needed. Indeed, Vargas had been the one to tell Espinal about Herrera's sudden passing.

Espinal believed that the sanctuary movement had taken its toll on Herrera, who took on full-time responsibilities on behalf of the two mothers living in confinement. "It was a lot of stress for him, too. If he was stressed or tired, I urged him to turn off his cell phone and get some rest. This is going to go on for a long time—we can't know for how much longer. The important thing is not to let it make you sick. He told me he would take care of himself and take breaks, but I think maybe he wasn't doing that."

What Do We Do?

For Pasquarello and fellow Columbus activists, the actual event of Herrera's passing would be indelibly connected to the untimely and tragic death of their friend and fellow activist Amber Evans. At the age of twenty-eight, Evans had been working for the Juvenile Justice Coalition in Columbus, Ohio, for four years. In January of 2019, she was promoted to executive director, and while she loved many aspects of her job, the shift from organizing and doing grassroots work to becoming an administrator conducting grasstops activities made her feel sidelined.

On Monday, January 28, Evans left work after a 5:30 p.m. meeting, informing her coworkers she was feeling poorly. At 6:30 p.m., she was seen on the security footage of a local store, where she purchased cold medicine and a Snickers bar. After the footage that showed her leaving the store, she was not seen again.

On Saturday, March 23, a body recovered from the Scioto River in Columbus, Ohio, was identified as belonging to Evans. Examiners verified that she had toxic levels of diphenhydramine and acetaminophen in her system when she died, and her death was considered a suicide. A text message she had sent to her mother, Tonya Fischer, on the day she disappeared simply read, "I love you, I'm sorry."[31]

Herrera and Pasquarello attended her service on April 5, 2019.

On the day following the service, spring began to yield the season's first hint of pleasant weather—the kind that sends gardeners skipping outside to enjoy the sun's warmth and begin the tasks related to spring clean-up. Herrera had been animated and vibrant, happy to be getting outside again. His garden centered him.

Pasquarello had been sitting in the living room, studying for his evidence class while a March Madness game played on their TV. Herrera floated through, moving in and out of the house, working here and there. The television was placed in front of the window, so Pasquarello wasn't entirely aware of what Herrera was getting into on the front porch. He didn't recall the last time Herrera walked by—it had been entirely uneventful. About ten minutes went by, but this, too, was nothing remarkable. It was such a nice day. Herrera was probably absorbed in his outdoor tasks.

Suddenly, Pasquarello heard a strange voice coming through the back door, announcing the Columbus police.

"I'm like, 'What the fuck?' And then I come out . . . and I'm seeing the ambulance. I forget exactly what he said . . . something like, 'Do you live here?'"

An emergency vehicle was in the alley behind their home where, as Pasquarello observed when he exited the back door and crossed the yard, Herrera had collapsed. Their neighbor Ashley had been the one to spot him, and he saw that she was crying. She went straight to Pasquarello and hugged him.

"I was just in shock. He's lying there unresponsive. . . . I think they were just trying CPR on him for a while, and I just crouched down beside the ambulance. And then I remember my neighbor Becky from across the street. She showed up and I think she was trying to be as positive as possible. She was saying, 'He's gonna be fine.'"

Eventually, Herrera was placed on a stretcher and attached to a machine that continued the chest compressions. At that point, Pasquarello and his neighbors were holding onto the hope that Herrera could still be revived. "But I feel like when I saw that machine press down on his chest so hard . . . ," Pasquarello trailed off.

As I listened to him describe these events, even though I was completely aware of the outcome of the emergency measures taken by the team of first responders, a part of me hoped that Herrera could still be revived, as though the power of Pasquarello's retelling *this* time could lead to a different outcome.

Ashley drove Pasquarello to the nearby Mount Carmel Hospital while he reached out to Ruben Jr. to come meet them. Once there, Pasquarello was quickly pulled into a side room by hospital personnel, and he took this to be a bad sign.

"He was pronounced dead on arrival. They couldn't do anything. And so a doctor came in and said it very quickly. I knew. I knew it was about to happen, but I was refusing to accept it. Then, when the doctor came and said it, I just kind of shattered." Sudden cardiac arrest was the cause of death, which had occurred despite a total lack of the usual warnings such as chest pains, dizziness, nausea, or breathlessness. The most common warning symptom is chest pain that lasts from twenty minutes to ten hours before the cardiac arrest. In other words, Herrera had no complaints on the day of his passing, just a steady smile for Pasquarello and a spring in his step to match April's brightening rays.

Ruben Jr. soon appeared. He and Pasquarello were asked if they wanted to see the body, and they both did. It felt like the natural thing to do for them, so they were escorted to Herrera's side. It fell to Ruben Jr. to inform his sisters of the tragedy, but because they were all located outside of Ohio, it would take some time for them to arrive. Pasquarello and Ruben Jr. sat together at the side of Herrera who was now—suddenly and outrageously—his body without his life within.

"I don't know how long we were there. I think we were there at least four or five hours."

Pasquarello recalled feeling angry at a woman on the hospital staff who he had to interact with. In retrospect, he understood that she had the very difficult job of working with loved ones during one of the worst experiences of their lives. When she came to check on them, Pasquarello said she seemed surprised that they were still in the room with Herrera's body, and he was taken aback by that. As he described it:

> Where the fuck else would I be right now? I mean, I had anger, among many other emotions, and I felt like I had to direct that somewhere. I was like, "Fuck this woman." She had to do the necessary, but ridiculous, thing of having us sign papers. I think it was Ruben [who had to sign]. Because I'm not a legal relative or anything. We weren't married. . . . So she was that person who was doing the hard work of saying, "Yes, it's hard, but we have some forms you have to sign."[32]

By the time Pasquarello left Mt. Carmel, again with their neighbor Ashley, it was late at night. He was struck hard by the sight of their front porch when he neared their home.

"One thing I saw when I came to the house was the front porch. It was cleaned up and beautiful and pristine. I lost it when I saw that."

On the last day of his life, Herrera had been cleaning and organizing their spacious front porch—the perfect reflection of his own joy in spring's new life. Pasquarello hadn't seen it before that moment because he had been studying and glancing at the basketball game in the living room while Herrera gardened, and then he had exited through the back alley after Herrera's collapse. He spent the night at Ashley's, where he called his parents, who drove through the night to arrive the next morning to be with their son in his time of grief.

On April 8, two days following Herrera's death, the team that supported Miriam Vargas gathered at her place of sanctuary at the First English Lutheran Church and found her overcome with emotion. Even though she met with them as usual, she could only manage a few words. "He was like my father," she said. "He was like a grandfather to my daughters."[33]

Both Espinal and Vargas knew that their champion had left many strategies and action plans in place that others could follow. There were entire congregations and activist organizations that were there to fight for them, but there really was not another individual who had provided them with the steady conviction and affection that had stoked the inner strength they needed to become leaders of the sanctuary movement.

As Vargas struggled to regain composure and resume her struggle as a voice for undocumented mothers in the weeks following his death, she told the *Columbus Free Press*, "Rubén was always texting me early in the morning, asking 'What do you need?' . . . He gave me strength every single day. He was my angel. I always told him that. He would always say, 'I'm just here to help.'"[34]

You Just Got Promoted

> Although the grief associated with the loss of Rubén is still fresh, I also want to emphasize that this has caused a shock to the organizing ecosystem in Columbus. . . . I'm asking today that anyone who has been involved on the periphery of immigrant rights organizing sit up and take note: you just got promoted.
>
> —Austin Kocher, Facebook Post, April 12, 2019

In the days, weeks, months, and years following Herrera's passing in April of 2019, organizers, activists, and progressive leadership in the City of Columbus still grapple with the question of what to do with the void he left. Sentiments such as organizer Austin Kocher's "you just got promoted" are raised alongside the acknowledgement that Herrera's departure leaves a space that cannot be truly filled.

On the cold and snow-covered day of Thursday, February 18, 2021, ICE officers granted Espinal an order of supervision that allowed her to safely leave sanctuary after forty months. On Tuesday, February 23, 2021, Miriam Vargas, accompanied by her attorney and a group of supporters, met with ICE agents at their field office and, like Espinal, went from being a priority for deportation to being placed under an order of supervision that allowed her to leave sanctuary at First English Lutheran Church and return to her family home on the southwest side of Columbus.[35] Lizbeth Mateo, Espinal's attorney, credited Biden's administration with new guidelines that limited who could be arrested and deported.[36] Each of them had weathered Herrera's passing while in confinement, followed by the COVID-19 pandemic that resulted in an even deeper experience of isolation as church congregants could no longer gather for worship in the spaces that housed them.

"Me duele mucho no haber podido despedirme," Espinal told me. ("It really hurts not to have been able to say goodbye.") She continued:

> Siento que faltó más convivencia. . . . A veces creo que no tomé mucho en cuenta de su presencia. Cuando yo bajaba a las 10, a las 11 de la mañana él ya estaba allí. No me daba cuenta que él estaba para apoyarme, que él estaba para mí. Incluso cuando mi hijo se accidentó, él fue el primero en llegar al hospital. Se hizo pasar por su tío y lo visitó. Siempre. Los dos siempre estaban. Cuando Nick no estaba en la escuela estaba allí . . . Faltó más. Hubo mucho más que decir. Mucho más que celebrar. Esto iba a ser algo que íbamos a celebrar juntos.[37]

When Herrera lost his mother to cancer when he was only four years old, it defined his life. The final campaign to which he had been fervently devoted was that of fighting to keep Edith Espinal and Miriam Vargas united with their children. When he and his siblings became migrants, losing not only their ties to their mother but to the entire Castilla family when they left Texas to start life anew in Oregon, a seed of empathy for the real-life impacts of family separation was planted. It seemed to me that Herrera's last act of service was an elegant tribute to Pura Castilla and the maternal love whose absence always weighed heavily in his life.

When I interviewed Naomi Chamberlain in April of 2022, I asked her the type of question that felt feeble and rote when presented to Herrera's nearest kin. She answered it as gamely and graciously as she could.

"What would he have considered to be one of his most important victories or successes?" I asked.

After pausing to reflect, Naomi offered:

> I think it would be peace. In one of my last conversations with him, he talked about how he was happy and just really fulfilled in his relationship with Nick. He just felt comfortable. . . . And it speaks volumes, because I think he was searching for so long and I can relate with having the type of brain that never shuts off. Finding peace in that storm is so hard.[38]

Naomi's comment made me think of Amber Evans and a conversation I had with Herrera when Evans had been reported missing for over a month. He confided that her inner circle of family and friends were acknowledging among each other how burnout and despair were a constant threat to activists who were always situated in the darkest corridors of humanity's capacity for cruelty.

I thought, too, about Herrera's urgency to conduct grassroots campaigns as a servant of the people rather than positioning himself at the helm of an established organization's administrative hierarchy. At times, when procedural regularity became a priority, his contributions as a maverick catalyst were met with some irritation on the part of his collaborators. I also discovered, in the process of speaking with Herrera's family members and friends, how much Pasquarello had contributed to his ability to stay engaged at the grassroots level, when activists like Evans were forced to turn their passion for listening and engaging with people into administrative roles in order to make a living. The Colectivo Santuario, rather than being the cause for his heart failure, helped to keep him connected and engaged at the grassroots level, which is where he always wanted to be.

In October of 2022, I visited the Columbus Mennonite Church, where Espinal had been in sanctuary for over three years. I learned that the newest addition of their hymnal, *Voices Together*, includes a new liturgy dedicated to sanctuary that had been contributed by Rev. Miller and translated by Herrera with consultation from Andrea de Ávila and Christina Horst. Although the printed numbering indicated that it was liturgy number 1042, this number was crossed out, and a small ceremony was held to affix the number 1235 on top: the number of days Espinal had spent in sanctuary at Columbus Mennonite Church.

"Liturgy ~~1042~~ 1235"

God our sanctuary,	Dios nuestro santuario,
Grant us	concédenos a nosotros
and our neighbors near and far	y a nuestros vecinos
courage in our hearts,	cercanos y lejanos
peace in our homes,	valentía en nuestros corazones
and justice in our streets. Amen.	paz en nuestros hogares,
	y justicia en nuestras calles. Amén.[39]

The way Rev. Miller described it, creating sanctuary, as Herrera had done with his final campaign, meant creating a protected space for the sacred. When Herrera died, he left a huge open space that he had occupied in his life. In the wake of Herrera's death, a friend told Rev. Miller, "Maybe it's better for that space just to be open for a while, rather than rushing to fill it." Maybe the space that Herrera had occupied in his life and through his work is, itself, a sacred space—a sanctuary. "And so, we get to see the creation of that space itself as a gift," said Rev. Miller. "And we get to occupy that, not in the way that Rubén did, . . . but we get to find our way into it . . . as a sanctuary for anyone who comes into that space that he occupied."[40]

In the years I knew him, Herrera was eternally overbooked, so he wouldn't always be able to make it to an appointment. I recall that we were seated in his colorful living room once when this happened. Our discussion about food activism and the plans we were making for our Taco Reparations Brigade intervention to be held at Condado Tacos in 2019 went longer than we had anticipated. He ended up texting someone to let them know he wasn't going to make it. He regretted not being able to attend their function, but he had a phrase that he seemed to draw on whenever he felt self-conscious about being a no-show: "You're not that fucking important, Rubén."

Apparently, this YNTFI sentiment had been imparted by an early mentor or advisor, and it's not meant as a put-down at all. Instead, it was spoken in order to resist an individualistic way of imagining that we are in charge or in control. It's so easy to feel that people are extremely disappointed in us if we show up late or don't manage to show up at all. But from the tone of his comment, it was clear he was trying to disrupt this egocentric way of looking at his participation in a given event. "Life goes on without me being there" might be another way to express it.

From the archive of my personal experience leading community theatre projects with Spanish-speaking community members in Ohio, the phrase "trust the circle" has held special power. With my Ohio State University colleagues Ana Puga, Katey Boreland, and Moriah Flagler, I helped conduct Be the Street, a theatre and storytelling workshop held at the Our Lady of Guadalupe Catholic Social Services Center and other places throughout the West Side.

The participants at the Guadalupe Center were largely migrant women and men with little experience in the arts, and they had almost zero experience with performing. Nonetheless, they were excellent at jumping into theatre games and exercises and drawing on their own lives to create compelling performances that communicated both the joy and sorrow of migrant experience. The exercises, typical of theatre games, often found us stepping outside of our comfort zones and coming up with sounds and movements that were often nonsensical and/or patently silly.

One woman in the group had been very reluctant about participating in such an exercise. While our small group was huddled together preparing our scene, I found myself searching for the right words to offer encouragement. On a whim, I said, "Confía en el círculo. No estás sola." ("Trust the circle. You're not alone.") I saw her take in the words and watched as the expression on her face changed from anxiety to determination. She wasn't doing something alone, for herself. She was doing something with—and *for*—all of us. Our whole group. She suddenly felt she had permission to take up space and extend beyond her individual limits. She took a powerful step outside her comfort zone and into collective purpose and courage.

Herrera had RSVP'd that he was coming to the public performance of Be the Street that featured the intrepid Guadalupe Center participants. He was on the list of attendees but not in attendance. It turned out that the day would coincide with his memorial service on April 13, 2019, so he had a pretty solid excuse.

Even so, I saw him reflected in the performance of the young woman who had been too afraid to join our theatre games until it occurred to me to invoke the power of the circle—*his* circle. Following the performance, she took me aside to say, "Esto me ayudó a superar el miedo en mi corazón." ("This helped me overcome the fear in my heart.")

You *are* TFI, Rubén.

Punto.

HASTA LA VICTORIA SIEMPRE

A Trust the Circle Mix Tape

Kevin Zamora and Catalina Parra, courtesy of Dkéama Alexis.

"Hasta la Victoria siempre" was the expression that Rubén Castilla Herrera chose to have inked on his forearm, encircled by the ensō symbol. The brush-painted circle in Zen Buddhism represents the idea of completion and enlightenment, but it just as readily represents imperfection and that which is incomplete. The brushstroke reveals the uneven whisk of fibers across the surface: a singular brushstroke that allows for no modifications or do-overs. An unfinished swish of the brush, impossible to replicate, imperfect yet complete, just as it is.

The contents of the Trust the Circle Mix Tape are just that. There is no compendium of recollections about Herrera that can be exhaustive or definitive. The texts gathered here are like the ensō's uneven fibers gracefully sweeping across blank space: an organic collection of voices and conversations that could not have been readily summarized within the body of this book's chapters but that together serve as a tribute to how Herrera upheld a multivocal and open approach to community building.

Facebook Posts

The following posts are drawn from Herrera's Facebook profile. They were not selected with an eye toward organization or curatorial flair. Instead, they were hastily cut and pasted to serve as placeholders in my process of trying to piece together a timeline for this book—more as a way to orient myself than to reconstruct or summarize his social media posts. Eventually, Facebook removed access to his page, and, since they had not been legally married, Pasquarello was unable to retrieve them. The collection of posts I copied from his timeline became one of the only places where Herrera's unedited Facebook thoughts are gathered. Since he used social media to share his musings frequently, it felt appropriate to archive them here. Many posts dealt with politics, but plenty were simply windows onto how he felt about life—micro check-ins that invited communication and play. They are arranged from the most recent, which he wrote on the last day of his life, to the earliest post in 2010, which was simply the phrase, "Always trust the circle!"

April 6, 2019

Columbus Friends:

Anyone know where I can get a bale of hay? Even half a bale would be okay. My chickens are asking for it.

November 3, 2018

Today, the spiritual sacred of the Día de los Muertos met the secular sacred of Ohio State football on the campus of The Ohio State University. It was a moment I had been waiting for as long as I have been in Ohio.

And I was assured of where I belong.

October 28, 2018

Nicholas Pasquarello just said Flarda for Florida. I was like what????

October 27, 2018

The best tacos have:
Cilantro, 21 votes
Lettuce, 0 votes

October 23, 2018

Those moments when I hear, see and feel the goodness of people and life, even through individual and collective struggle. Today this happened in various ways and I realized it while walking to the car on this beautiful, clear, blue sky, sunny, cool, fall day. It struck me like a baptism of gratefulness, comfort, hope, newness and rebirth. And it brought me to tears.

October 22, 2018

Mine is a community of difference.
And therefore it is fragmented, ever changing and temporary.
Always temporary.
And that's how I like it.
Besides, no one belongs to only one community.
Not even my cats.
They hang with rodents, marsupials, humans and ghosts.

October 21, 2018

This is [my] question and I'm asking for peoples thoughts here:

What is the state of organizing or the state of play in change after the mass mobilization on the streets that happened after Trump was elected?

What is our story of now?

October 18, 2018

Art of Hosting Conversations vs. Art of Doing

June 19, 2018

Yesterday, after a news interview, three immigrant women mothers prayed with us outside on the hottest day of the year. They prayed for all families, for children, for the City of Columbus, for this country and for all of those addressing the cruelty of this administration. They also thanked God for all that is still good in the world and asked for the strength to continue loving and doing what they can to survive and serve others.

I cried as I left that circle of prayer. It's the women and the mothers who will save this world. I will humbly stand with them.

April 18, 2018

"Kitchen Table" Issues in my community:

—Long time residents being evicted
—High rent
—Homeless looking for a place to eat and sleep
—Opioid crisis
—Prostitution as the only source of income
—My neighbors being shot and robbed
—No nearby grocery store
—Seeing police officers and feeling they're not here to protect us
—Immigrants being separated from their families
—"Refugees" living here while their child or parent is in a refugee camp in another continent.
—An inadequate bus system
—A hospital that has served the community is leaving
—The rise of expensive condos/apartments and breweries blocking the view of the rise of infant and maternal mortality.
—Poor black, brown, white communities criminalized and incarcerated

—Walking down the street and someone yelling at me: "Go back to Mexico."

—Upperclass Queer elite orgs who disregard queer POC and the transgender.

—A woman whose only option to stay with her family is to be in sanctuary, not able to leave a church.

June 17, 2017

Queer activists of color arrested for protesting against police brutality at the Columbus Pride Parade. Police used force, mace, and tasers on the protesters. They are currently being held at the Franklin County Courthouse. NO STATEMENT FROM STONEWALL COLUMBUS OR PRIDE COMMITTEE YET!?? REMEMBER WHAT STONEWALL IS ABOUT!!!!

March 12, 2017

What if our homes became safe spaces, sanctuary spaces, spaces of resistance for those new and old, black, white or brown, queer, straight, CIS gendered, for ourselves . . . all those who just need a place to sleep for the night. What could we do then?

Tell me that story.

March 5, 2017

Sanctuary as holistic. Centering of oneself.
Belonging. Feeling joy. Experiencing love. Full respect.

Being able to say I'm Black, Brown, Woman, Undocumented, Queer, Trans, I am a child, elderly, I am beautiful, I am liberated . . . and I'm going to make it.

December 22, 2017

This tree was given to us. I haven't put up a tree for years and I set it up outside because we have no room inside. What we realized is that this decorated tree has become a symbol of sorts of community. People pass by and pause for a second and look at it or they will make a comment. People who I do not know but people with names and stories and families and struggles. Like me.

This tree belongs outside not inside. #TheBottoms

October 2, 2017

Espinal's daughter and son pleaded with authorities not to split the family up. Her daughter Stephanie said ICE left them no choice other than sanctuary after they had Edith buy a one-way ticket to Mexico for Oct. 10. "We don't want her to leave. We don't want to be separated as we were before. I just cannot imagine not having my mom next to me, it has been really hard. I see my mom stressed out, not knowing what is going to happen next." —Stephanie Espinal.

November 6, 2016

Thanks to all who joined in the circle yesterday as we collectively shared ourselves, our story and those that we have lost. It was a sacred space for conversation on LIFE, DEATH, HEALING, LOVE and FORGIVENESS

February 1, 2016

It's beautiful what one encounters on the path of life. But you have to truly feel what you see. You have to love but more difficult, allow yourself to be loved. One must be surrounded with an inner circle of people who love, support and accept you at your best and at your not so best. You have to find space for centering, self reflection, community and a place to dance. Differences become strengths and learning spaces; communication becomes a practice and loving unconditionally is much about deconstructing learned behavior . . . fighting for justice, liberty and liberation with the people is a must. Always in the present. So it is for me.

Thank you friends and family. I bow to you. Four year anniversary month with my friend and partner Nicholas Pasquarello.

No hay balas que penetren la fuerza de éste amor.

October 15, 2015

WOW! I just spent 6+ hours with Guillermo Gomez-Peña from La Pocha Nostra and several other CompañerX on a workshop on Art and Activism at Ohio State University. What a day! Lots of Radical compassion, self-reflection, communication, collaboration, community building, silence, human performance theater and experimental theater.

June 11, 2015

PRIDE MONTH IS REAL

Every time I put something out in public about being Latinx and Gay/Queer and the power of liberation, I receive a private, sometimes anonymous note with a question, a struggle, a story, a thank you or a show of support. It is here where liberation lies. I thank my brother Ramón

Herrera for this. He was my inspiration in all that I am and all I do. Someday, we will all be free. I may not know when it will be but someday, we will all be free.

September 28, 2014

Always Trust the Circle—#tomatillos brought the bees to the #garden! Yay! #love #urbangarden #neareastside #columbusohio #trustthecircle

June 3, 2013

"Tinkerers" have skills but no clear plan. We know that analytic plans and metrics drive us to what we think we already know. We make do with the resources at hand. We open space to what's possible in the moment. We tinker towards messy complex systems because it takes a lot of repeated messes until something workable emerges. We see messes as diverse creativity. We seek order in a disorderly way until something new emerges. When this happens, you keep tinkering. Because life is a circle, not a line.

August 7, 2012

Gerardo: I'm a queer undocumented Mexican. We exist. We're involved. #QueerLatino #NoPapersNoFear #UndocuBUS

April 19, 2010

Today I pause, ring the bell, breathe and observe a moment of silence to honor my sister Ruth who left this world a year ago today. She helped me know myself better and finally know my mother. In her last words to me she asked me to remember our family circle. Thank you Ruth for helping heal our family lineage. This alone gives me hope and courage in my personal healing and for the healing of the world.

February 1, 2010

Always trust the circle!

Rubén Castilla Herrera's Organizing Tips

by Nick Torres

Who are you, and why are you here?

Rubén had a certain way of transforming a question with just the right combination of sincerity, optimism, and urgency. "Who are you, and why are you here?" He frequently posed this question as an introduction before a training or group facilitation. Then he would pause and repeat the question, opening his arms wider and wider each time to suggest a series of concentric circles: "That could mean why are you here? . . . Why are you *here*? . . . Or why are you **HERE**?" (arms open to the heavens, elevating slightly onto the balls of his feet for emphasis).

There is power in the invitation. Whoever comes is supposed to be here.

Intersectionality was fundamental to Rubén's vision for equity and justice. Rubén would always meet you where you were. You didn't have to be a seasoned activist. You showed up that day, and that mattered. You had purpose. He thoughtfully and diligently built community with everyday people because he believed that your struggles were his struggles.

There is always something you can do.
Respect yourself, respect each other, and respect this place.

Rubén would say that his time as a migrant farm laborer left a strong impression on his work ethic as an organizer. He was efficient and disciplined, always intentional with his actions—whether planting and pruning his bountiful garden or sowing and nurturing the seeds of social justice movements.

May his life's work continue to inspire our collective efforts to create a world that truly appreciates the inherent dignity and agency of each person.

Hasta la victoria.

Nick Torres
c/s[1]

Rubén Castilla Herrera's Organizing Tips

1. Only do it if you believe it.
2. This is not a job.
3. Respect yourself, respect others, respect this place.
4. Be your message. Wear your message.
5. Just do what is right for the community.
6. Don't do it by yourself.
7. It's okay to say no.
8. Always have an invite and ask.
9. Surround yourself with people smarter than you.
10. Find a teacher.
11. Don't take yourself so f*n' serious.
12. When you're frustrated, stand back.
13. Check in, check out, debrief.
14. Arrive early.
15. Be creative.
16. Breathe, rest, balance.
17. Go to the community.
18. Intersect.
19. Read.

20. Listen more than you talk.
21. Don't give into desire and fear.
22. Whoever shows up are those who need to be there.
23. Diversity and Inclusion always.
24. Create chaos with order.
25. Space creates power, power creates space.

Safe Spaces, Police Brutality, and Recollections of a Sucker Punch: The West Side Identity of Rubén Castilla Herrera

an interview with Paloma Martinez-Cruz

I interviewed Herrera for a research project on placemaking on Columbus's West Side on August 17, 2017. We sat outdoors on a warm summer day on Parsons Avenue and ate ice cream from a local shop. I was interested in learning about his West Side identity and his life as an organizer in Columbus. I especially wanted to understand how he had come to make Ohio his home, as I myself was in the process of making sense of what it meant to be based in Columbus. He was an obvious person to turn to: I considered him to be among the best things the city had to offer.

Paloma Martinez-Cruz: All right, Rubén. So I wanted to ask you some questions about experiences of the West Side. Can you tell me about what you do? First of all?

Rubén Castilla Herrera: Yeah, I work with the Central Ohio Worker Center. It's a call center that is a continuation of immigrant justice work that we've been doing. I never know how to say it. Immigrant rights? Immigrant justice? It's working with immigrants and migrants, and also with worker issues that involve nonimmigrants, people who live here, Black, White, Brown, new Americans, refugees, whatever the terminologies are. So it's more of a diverse crowd, but also, how that intersects with liberation for all people. . . . That's that we're always trying to navigate those diverse spaces through individual cases but also through the collective familia. That's what feels natural, feels real. But it's still difficult. Still challenging.
PMC: What feels natural and what feels challenging?
RCH: A veces quiero llorar, right? I just want to cry. To cry can come from joy, but it also could come from anger, or just beauty, right? When you're dealing with people, it's just hard. Yesterday, for example . . . there's this older man, estábamos con un señor, that was stopped by a police officer. Undocumented. He found our number—we have a Rapid Response Hotline. This man was scared because he got a ticket. A driving ticket. He was literally scared for his life. He wanted some assistance, and we connected him to an attorney. But more than that, I feel his cry was of ¿Qué voy a hacer? What am I going to do? What can happen here?

To me, even as a person con papeles, who has papers, that's from here, I feel that way also. It's the same only different. And I'm feeling that way more and more during these times. Sometimes I just want to talk to people. I just want to check in because I want to ask: What do I do? So that's hard. That's challenging.

So being on the West Side, that can answer your question. You know, we're kind of more connected with that in the sense that you see it, you see it walking down the street. It's not just Brown people or migrants or immigrants. It's poor White people, it's prostitutes down Sullivant Avenue, people that are addicted to some kind of drug, and it's really people asking, "What do I do?" And they ask it in different ways. Sometimes they ask for money. By ignoring you.

I think once you're in tune to that, to my experience, then there's no way to untune it. You're really in tune with it. And so that's the challenge.

PMC: Can you tell me where you're from originally?

RCH: Yeah, I was born in Texas. Tejano. And even that, what is a Tejano? Is it Mexicanness, my grandparents and my parents, and the language and the loss of language and gaining it back. And all the identity politics: how will we identify and how people are identified.

I grew up as a migrant farmworker in California, Oregon, Washington, which was another part of the role, right? So, it was that experience and we settled in Oregon, but I came to Ohio and I lived in Ohio most of my life now.

PMC: How old were you when you came to Ohio?

RCH: Gosh, I guess I was twenty-eight.

PMC: Okay. Do you want to say how old you are now?

RCH: Not really.

PMC: You said, "most of your life." So maybe if you told me we could do a little math.

RCH: That question. I need to get over that, right? And I just can't. Why can't I just say who I am? What am I running from? So, that's another conversation.

PMC: I'm interested in those basic conversations about who you are, though. You're a really good person to reflect with on those meanings. How do you feel when people ask you where you're from? How do we identify? What's at stake?

You're Chicano in Ohio and making spaces for new voices, but meanwhile you're explaining everything around that. What do these questions mean to you? What's your identity in Ohio and on the West Side?

RCH: That's interesting, because I came here on the bus and there was a bit of a delay downtown. Two women asked me that same question. Complete, liberal White, they were seemingly White. And I generally don't like to generalize, I'm a little bit bothered by that. But, once you've been asked a lot of times you, you really know kind of where it's coming from. And sure enough, what I thought was coming happened. It's like, "Oh, she was wanting to practice her Spanish." She thought I was Hispanic or Latino or whatever. And then it was an opportunity for her to practice her Spanish, which I was fine with, because, you know, I find that's almost entertaining, in a sense. But with that came other assumptions, which was interesting.

Because my stereotype of her was, I thought, they're probably Jehovah's Witness, just by the way they were dressed and just my experience, and I was right! But it didn't start that way. They were actually pretty smooth. They were talking about our commonalities and things like that, and then they asked me how my day was. How your day is going is a good question.

I told them how this morning I was working in my garden, because that's how I how center myself. And I said, "We have family coming." I told them I was painting my deck because we had family coming. And then she jumped into something very interesting. She said, "Is your wife going to be cooking a lot of Mexican food?" With no other information.

First of all, I'm queer. I don't have a wife, I have a partner and his name is Nick. You know him. So, that's one. And the other is the assumption was my wife was going to be cooking and that she was Mexican. That reminded me of something that may have happened to me somewhere else years ago.

PMC: Wait! Don't go to something from years ago! Tell me what you said on the bus! I need to know.

RCH: In this case, you know, there's battles you just don't fight, and I just didn't have time. I just said, "No." And then honestly, I drifted away from that and went to this Black woman that was like upset. Because the bus wasn't there. I just felt drawn to that. I wanted to hear her pain.

PMC: So, you left the Jehovah's Witness party and went over to where there was some rage.

RCH: Yeah, yeah. I didn't do it rude. But it was kind of, "Oh, wow," and then I faded her out. That was really interesting. So those kinds of experiences are more likely to happen, I think, in Columbus, Ohio, right now. But I don't know, maybe not. But the question was, you wanted to know what had been said, right? If I would have been on the street, demonstrating at a protest, I might have thought, "What the fuck? What do you mean by that?" I would have confronted, but in that situation, I didn't feel that's what I wanted to do. Let it go. Just fade it out.

So I have these encounters, and turning back the community, to the West Side. I used to live in this part of town, [Olde Towne East], and we got gentrified out.

PMC: What was happening that made you notice the changes?

RCH: It's interesting. It's called Olde Towne East and, and Olde Towne is a gentrified name because you know, the O-L-D-E T-O-W-N-E.

PMC: It's a Renaissance Fair.

RCH: Exactly. We refuse to call it Olde Towne. The community that lived here longer calls it the Near Eastside, which is a big area. . . . And so where I live now is kind of West Franklinton, closer to the Hilltop. The people that mostly live there have moved there in the last forty to fifty years and are elderly, poor White, poor Black, and then new Hispanic Latino families coming in.

PMC: What does it mean when you think about your community where you live?

RCH: The great thing about that space is that those houses still have porches. And there's people that have porches and no air-conditioning. We have air-conditioning and it operates great, but so many people are still outside in their porches, and so I'm starting to get to know people.

The first part of Columbus people come to, that's usually where people will settle. And so lots of people came from Chicago, from California, or from somewhere in the West. . . . For me, there are more and more markers that remind me of who I am, as a proud person who is Latinx, as Latino, that I feel like I'm a little closer to that, even if it's a billboard, or, more likely to see someone in a passing car playing norteño or some kind of music. Those kind of little reminders, cultural reminders, are important for me. And help me survive, I think, and feel connected in a really interesting way. They may not be my story completely, but they still connect me.

PMC: In the advocacy work that you do, are you hearing narratives that are different? Since the 2016 Trump agenda? Do you see a difference in how Spanish speakers feel? Noticing?

RCH: Before the election, people were asking, "¿Qué va a pasar si Trump gana?" And they say, "No va a ganar." And then it happened, people were really scared, and for some people that turned into, "We're leaving." Or at least mentally leaving. Like, "I have to think about leaving." And there's some people that actually left, but most stayed. The need to provide for family is greater even than Trump. And therein lies the hope, and hopefully the fight.

The DACA students are concerned. I think most of them still live with their parents. . . . And you're worried about them, and you're also trying to function as a young person. I don't think there's enough spaces for people to talk about that. Our initial conversation is how do we, how can we let people know that it's okay, how can we create a safe space, and we can even laugh about it? Or not laugh? But laughter isn't just laughing.

PMC: To take some refuge in our mutual understanding. And be free to see the absurdity in it.

RCH: Yeah, the absurdity.

PMC: Do you identify any spaces as being safe spaces? Spaces that work like that on the West Side?

RCH: So it starts by talking to each other, and where I come from, we're community people and we laugh and we share our pain, and we have to be there for each other. I'm fortunate enough to work with a group of people where that's what we do. But it's not a job for me, that's who I am. . . . But it's a very slow process. And it's not something that if I saw it on the chart, it would be impressive on a corporate graph.

So the question now is, how do we learn from each other? And how do we share? What I do now is connect people to resources that people have a right to. . . . But it seems now this is the lining, silver lining, if you will, it seems like the there's been more since the inauguration. There have been more people, diverse people and allies that say, "What do I do? How can we help? "

PMC: I've been in the street with you in protest and I've heard about your organizing on pinche High Street. What would you say is the most unsafe you've felt in the street? And what is the opposite of that, maybe what's the safest you've felt in the street in your activist work?

RCH: Well, the unsafe comes to mind in the literal sense. One time we went to, to collect wages for a Hispanic man that was a painter. We actually went to the company. We went with a group of people because we never go in on our own. The vice president came, and he got so upset that he literally punched me, hit me.

PMC: How many were you?

RCH: It was about ten or twelve, including the person whose wages we were trying to collect. I just came in as support. And so there's been that. And that was so unexpected and quick. It was just hard to really process all at once. And it was just so surreal.

But in terms of demonstrations, I feel like now in Columbus, and I think it's indicative of the rest of the country, that the police state has increased their protection of the corporate state and they're increasing their tactics. Here in Columbus, first it was just police cars, then there was more police. And then they got bikes started—a few. And now at any demonstration, there's fifty, sixty, seventy bikes. And they use their bikes as weapons, right?

And then the horses show up with them. The horses, they're big animals, and they started pepper-spraying us. And then they started arresting us and detaining and beating us. And in some cases, not necessarily at protests, but they've killed us. So they've identified us as the true enemy. They're not letting up, and they're supported by every level of the system. . . . The public in general is still not understanding. And so the most danger I've felt is increasing.

Certainly the police state, I explained this earlier, I don't believe that they're here to protect and serve *me*. Or people like me, or people of color, or struggling people. They're here to move us out. Either through gentrifying or drug raids to moving out right? In the name of cleaning up the neighborhood. That's the danger I feel. It's a little bit more every day.

As far as safe, I think that interesting. I think ritual, when people sing together. There's something about a common setting where we all are doing something together. Singing or chanting in numbers where you feel each other and you realize in that moment that "I am doing the right thing for justice." I think overall, despite the dangers and the unsafety, and the hope for me is that those kind of moments, you feel you're really going to prevail. That's how we're going to get through this.

PMC: What's one of the songs that have made you feel that way?

RCH: There's a really beautiful song, especially when sung together: "We Who Believe in Freedom Cannot Rest." It's just powerful, and the words are believing and freedom. When I just heard it recently, it made me cry, actually. And it sustains me, I think, in the struggle.

But this does too, right? It's a conversation that I haven't had. And you know, we're out in the world in an open space and a few people said, "Hi," and that's believing in freedom, and that's not resting as well.

MenuFesto

by Paloma Martinez-Cruz

for Rubén Castilla Herrera

For starters we call for reparations for every brownface taco
modified by the words macho or mucho macho or macho nacho or nacho
mamma

We call for reparations for every brownface taco
that suggests something dirty gross or wrong as in
pink taco dirty taco wet taco illegal taco nacho cheese dorito loco taco
hairy biker's bandido taco chi-chi's foldables pocket taco dirty sanchez taco
and all things tuesday taco

And you can keep your mission position donations
this is no charity cotillion we're demanding reparations until all food is
fair food
can we get an órale

For the main course we want you to know we are not unaware of your
NAFTA flex
it's not lost on us how only hipsters can afford heirloom grade handmade
tortillas
while Indian people die from processed food obesity
brought to you by cheap commodity corn stuffed down throats
by Monocle Man of the North

Have you left room for just deserts? Fantastic let's roll in the cart:
we claim maíz as cultural patrimony and enchiladas as intellectual property
we call for reparations until bordered bodies circulate as freely as our burritos
until our children are as beloved as our chalupas
can we get an órale

We call for amnesty of our sacred corn and amnesty for all gente de maíz
not just the ones who have "done nothing wrong"
we want our straight A student but no less or more than the mother
who speaks no English and spells Spanish creatively
as when she switches out the B and the V or the G and the H: a guebo
(in English this means going toward egg
but in Chicanish you're saying by my testicle, yes)

You see, we want the homie with the felony conviction
the tamalera with her crooked sign
the grandfather with his gray pleather ankle boots from the pulga
tapping up and down the street like it's 1969
we are not parasites pathogens predators or monsters
we are a nation not an infestation
con safos por vida a guebo

An early version of this poem was first published in About Place Journal, *October 2020.*

Dear Rubén

by Pranav Jani

I was—and will always be—heartbroken that due to family responsibilities, I could not attend the memorial service for Rubén on April 13, 2019, or the march and gathering that followed it.

But what gives me solace is that I know, with 100 percent certainty, what Rubén would say to that: be with your family. Anytime my kids came to any protest or event, Rubén would be one of the few who would go up to them and talk to them, earnestly. These small gestures of intimacy always made me feel like a whole person, not just a fellow activist.

Beyond the many marches and rallies and organizing meetings we attended together since we first met in 2006, too many to count, this affection is what binds me to his memory, what makes me tear up as I write these words.

I tried to convey this feeling many of us have for Rubén in a letter I wrote to him after his passing and was thrilled beyond measure when I learned that Erin Upchurch, a tremendous activist and organizer in this city, would read it at the April 13 march. I am reprinting it here, but I also invite you to find Erin's powerful rendition as captured in a *Columbus Dispatch* video of the event.

Dear Rubén,

I wish you could see all the people who have gathered today, to celebrate your life.

I wish you could see all of us who have been inspired by you, moved by you, fed by you, educated by you, loved by you.

I wish you could see all of us who will always remember you and keep learning from you.

They say that a person never truly dies until the last person who remembers them is also gone.

From that point of view, you will certainly live forever.

My dear Rubén.

When I walked into 400 W. Rich Street in late January, joining dozens and dozens of people searching for our friend and sister Amber [Evans], supporting each other, being present for each other, I started playing the role I've become used to . . . the one who consoles others. The one who is there for others.

It was when I saw you, I realized I needed to be consoled. I needed support. And you hugged me and hugged me. And Tammy [Fournier-Alsaada] came and we hugged and hugged.

And I want to ask, who will console me now?

But your words of encouragement come back to me. We have each other, you said. We have to hold on to each other, for each other, you said.

We will carry on together, with you and Amber in our hearts.

Dear brother.

Here's what I learned from you yesterday.

I was watching your interview with Loose Films on why you love gardening. You talked about the joy you felt "to watch something grow, to water it, to nurture it, to pick it . . . to share it . . ."

And you said, in your humble and assuming and genuine way: "That's how I try to live my life, I guess."

You certainly organized that way: valuing the spontaneous growth of movements and groups and working with them as they grow and emerge.

In fact, the first use of the word "organize" in the English language is connected with the word "organic," to build something intimately tied to our bodies, our existence.

What if we organized like we were working in a garden together, growing new ideas and movements, nurturing them, sharing the results . . .

My dear brother, my comrade, my friend—

How many protests and rallies and meetings did we attend together?

How many people did you inspire with your unique, patient methods, connecting so many different struggles?

Look at the diversity of this crowd. How much do we owe the unity in Columbus across movements to your incessant work and inner conviction to speak truth to power?

You took the lead in organizing so many campaigns. Farmworkers justice. Defending undocumented immigrants. Organizing May Day so it was always multilingual and intersectional. Organizing around sanctuary in ways that included the Black community and fighting police brutality.

And yet working with everyone didn't mean watering down what you had to say. You didn't go for "unity at all costs" but you unified with people and lifted them to a new set of ideas.

For example. Always proclaiming, proud and unafraid, in every space that you are queer and Latinx and indigenous—creating and affirming space for your multiple identities.

For example. Always showing up to fight for Palestine. To take on Islamophobia. To question Democratic politicians. To question imperialism. To question capitalism at its very roots.

Dear Rubén,

It's finally spring. Even in Columbus, it finally had to happen.

The trees are starting to bloom. The clouds are even parting at times, with sunshine and warmth.

It feels like winter, with you gone. I have so many unfinished dialogues with you—and I need your guidance as I enter new phases in my life.

But I look at the flowers growing, and I feel your presence, and I start, ever so slowly, to turn over the soil and begin my garden again.

Love Shows Up: Reflections on Amber and Rubén

by Erin Upchurch

Not long after ending a conversation with Paloma about my friendships with Rubén and Amber, and about my thoughts for this book, I spent some time with my daughter getting updates on her first few weeks in college. Unexpectedly, our neighbor knocked on the door to share that a deer was foraging in our backyard. We hurriedly rushed into the kitchen, and out of the window, we indeed saw a sweet doe, or maybe a baby deer, gleefully munching on the brilliantly green leaves and overgrown grass. In all my years of suburban living, I'd never been this physically close to a deer. We stood mesmerized for what felt like an hour, though it was likely closer to ten minutes. There was a playfulness in our friend, a naivete, perhaps, in trusting that they'd be safe in the yard of a human at midday. We also observed their brazen quest for food. They seemed so hungry. Shortly after enjoying their meal, this sweet one walked slowly to a nearby tree and sat down to rest under the shade. Again, boldly trusting that they'd be okay.

In 2019, my dear friend, sister, and comrade Amber Evans died. Her life ended unexpectedly in that the community didn't necessarily see it coming. However, I can't say that it didn't make sense, as in the months prior to her death, she was observed to be both worn and weary. The last time I saw her, her eyes were dark and tired, devoid of their usual sparkle and twinkle of hope.

Sharing time and space with our deer reminded me of Amber. She had beautiful, brown doe eyes. Eyes that danced with joy. Playful. Serious. Earnest. Eyes that would often overflow with heartache and pain. Amber trusted in something or someone bigger than herself. She was a creative in her vision of a different kind of world being available to us all. She was nonnegotiable in her commitment to liberation but not necessarily freedom. Freedom gives permission to be in a space. Liberation is the space.

Amber's love for her people and ache for change seemed to create blind spots in her own life. Her friends and family knew her to be almost childlike in her play, yet super-serious in her work of social justice. Amber was hungry. Hungry for truth and justice. And while she was devoted in her zeal to feeding others, one might say she forgot to leave some for herself.

On a recent evening, my daughter shared with me a video of a deer that was in her friend's front yard as she was getting in her car to drive home. The deer was initially sitting and then stood up as she slowly drove by. It did not appear to be startled—it almost looked as if it had been waiting for her to arrive.

This was the feeling I had the moment Rubén Castilla Herrera entered my life. One day, he was just there, returning my gaze as though he had been expecting me. And then he was always there, anywhere and everywhere. He radiated reverence for life in both macro- and micro-ways. There was a grace and ease that exuded from his eyes and an unmistakable fire all his own. Rubén died on April 6, 2019, the day after Amber's funeral, where he and I had shared a church pew and took communion together.

Rubén's eyes were deep, serious, and soft. They held ancestor-like wisdom and were unwavering in their commitment to connecting with others and into the depths of the earth. He trusted life. There was a baby-blueish ring around his brown eyes. Like a sky filled with the promise of rain, Rubén's eyes overflowed with an insistent call to liberation. He was dangerously grounded in radical compassion. He was a teacher, sibling, friend, and the ultimate soft landing.

Interestingly, a deer has appeared in my yard two additional times; both of which were on the days I was specifically thinking about writing this reflection. One day, there were two confidently resting amongst the fresh fallen leaves. My daughter thinks that the deer she saw that evening with her friend was the same visitor to our backyard. Logic tells me that this is unlikely, but my deep knowing tells me that she could be correct. Nonetheless, these deer are outliers in the forest world. That they would get so close to humans and dare hold their ground upon the arrival of humans is an example of the curious and perhaps audacious ways both Amber and Rubén moved through the world. Both meek and large in their own ways, I miss the gentleness and courage with which they would hold the chaos—a constant in the fight for justice and liberation. I appreciate their presence. I know that they are in some ways still here, still fighting, and absolutely still loving.

Trust the circle.

Broad Street Methodist Church Memorial Service, April 13, 2019

Held at Broad Street United Methodist Church, the selected excerpts are from Nicholas Pasquarello, Rita Herrera, Naomi Chamberlain, and Marisa Herrera-Garverick. It was one of many other services and remembrances in 2019, including memorials at Columbus Mennonite Church and First English Lutheran Church, where Edith Espinal and Miriam Vargas were in sanctuary.

Nicholas Pasquarello

I've been with Rubén countless times when he's called to speak somewhere. Some event, some rally, some gala. Some class or something. It's funny because I think we all know that he had a way with words. I personally don't know anybody that has a way of words like he does. But he would always be nervous. No matter how much he spoke, and it just was like second nature to him, he was always thinking, "Oh, I have to do this class presentation. I'm not sure what I'm gonna do, what I'm gonna say, and he'd be thinking about it for like two or three days and would write out a bunch of stuff. And he would end up with something like this, basically. So this is what I'm going to say right now.

There's two things I really want everyone in this room to know. First, that I was his favorite. Second, and this is more important, is that *you* were his favorite. Every single one of you . . .

He said that to his family, of course. He said that to a lot of people, and he truly meant it. There's no one who could be as intentional as a man; he was so intentional about everything. So I'm trying to do a little bit of that.

Right now, what I'm wearing actually, the shirt, this blazer, this little flower right here from Nick Torres's wedding. This is exactly what Rubén was wearing when he spoke at his last big thing that he spoke at, which was as the keynote speaker of the National Association of Social Workers at a gala for Ohio social workers. He did this new thing that was really powerful. He actually built an altar in front, just ten minutes of silence and just building an altar. Kind of centering on ritual and reflection in that way.

I think it's awesome that, first of all, he didn't know he was the keynote speaker of the event. He told me he was speaking at some social work thing. And then Heather came to me one day, and she was inviting me to the gala, too, and said, "Rubén's to be our keynote!" And I said [to him later], "Why didn't tell me you're the keynote?" And he's like, "Oh, my God, I didn't know I was the keynote. I gotta prepare."

But just that, in itself. He was the keynote speaker at a big gathering for social workers. And Rubén was a social worker, for sure. He didn't have that degree. But he was a social worker. And so in this space of professional social workers that navigate this, they chose to honor *him*. He was the person that they wanted to lift up.

Similarly . . . he never went the ordination path . . . but he was a pastor. He talked about pastoral care a lot. And people really went to him as someone to speak with . . . just countless times. Every day, every week. . . .

He was just all of these things, and that's . . . how we met. . . . I was sort of a grungy, crungy undergrad at OSU. You know, fighting administration for workers' rights and everything. And of course Rubén would go to anything like that, so that's how we met. . . . It was very new for both of us. You know, I had just recently come out and Rubén had never had a partner, and, obviously, there was an age difference. So it was kind of clandestine for a while. We were kind of living in the shadows, and he was staying stuff like, "I'm this community organizer and people are going to . . . you know."

I would literally sneak him up to my room to avoid my roommate at the time. Bit by bit, people found out, and we found that, like, everyone loves us and nobody cared. And his family accepted me, and my family accepted him. But in the first couple of months that we were together, we were almost in some kind of trance like, like kind of obsessive. We just didn't want to . . . do anything besides be with each other. We thought it would wear off, but it never did. I want to, I just leave you all with that. To hold your loved ones tight. Don't let the moment pass where you can say, "I love you." Because we never did. I'll always have that.

Rita Herrera

Hey, my name is Rita Herrera, and I was his favorite. I want to start off with a chant that I know through my friends, or my chosen family, and I will say it, and if you guys want to repeat the words after me, we can sing it together.

We are circling. We're circling together
We are singing, singing our heart song
This is family, this is unity
This is celebration, this is sacred.

I just have a couple of stories. I didn't write anything, so I'm just going to talk. I'm not very good at this. When we came to Ohio, I was ten. My dad took me and my brother and my sister and we lived at the Methesco and I just remember weird little games he taught us. . . . He was just so good at making us laugh, and his favorite thing to do was lay in bed with all of us in the living room and we'd make a bed and we'd all lay together. And we would listen to him tell stories about his childhood. And they weren't all happy stories, but they were his truth. And in the end, we would beg for them, "Let's all lay in the living room together and tell stories!" He was the best at that.

Later on, I remember him searching, he always wanted to make sure he was around Brown people, and that was so important to him. At the time, there was really not a Latino community at all. And so we would travel to Toledo and he would take me with him. And we would go to bailes and he taught me how to dance. I was the dancing partner. And everybody would always ask us, "Is this your wife?" And I'd be like, "No! Oh my gosh, no, no!" And he would hold my hand and say, "Yes, this is my child bride." He thought it was funny.

But now I look back, and I'm so grateful for those experiences. Dancing with my dad and him making sure I knew our culture, and it was just so special.

I also have something that I wrote him on Facebook a little bit ago. I said, "I miss my father Rubén Castilla Herrera. Please come visit me." And he answered, "I reflected on your words for several minutes and heard your voice. It brought tears to my eyes. And like the magical story of a beautiful gem, I felt your spirit and beauty. May the distance between us be devoured by our love for each other. For those around us, and for the universe, I miss you too." He was so good at like leaving messages like that. All over the place. It's just so nice to know that he loved us so much. He never let us not know that. And I'll miss him. I love you, Dad.

Naomi Chamberlain

Hi, I'm Naomi. I just want to start off by thanking you all. Thanking Broad Street Church for letting us hold this special moment to celebrate my father. Thank you, Nick Torres, for sharing that about my dad. It was beautiful.

My dad, he would have been so uncomfortable right now. But he would be happy because even though he was uncomfortable, he loved this. So I can see him just smiling right now, his beautiful smile. Second, I want to take a second to thank my dad. My papa bear. My daddy. Thank you. Thank you for all the memories and lessons you provided me and every person you've touched.

I love you. I just want to take a second to share a few stories about my dad. My papa, my daddy. First, he was a caregiver, as you all know, and you've heard he moved here in 1987. I was only three, and he would take care of me. He would brush my hair, and he would braid it, and he just loved me like his baby.

I remember a time, a story that my dad took much pride in. It was picture day, where we lived in Delaware. I was in first grade, and we were in front of the school. He was brushing my hair, and he was braiding it. And he got strange looks. I mean, this was so rare, such a rare sight in the early nineties. A Latino man brushing his daughter's hair, fixing it for her pictures?

My dad, he loved those kinds of stories. He thrived on that. And he thrived on those looks that people would give them, and he shared that story. Those moments always made a good story for him. And he would always tell it, and we'd reflect on it, and we'd laugh. It's just something that I will always treasure.

He was loving. He always had sayings, like little silly sayings or something that he would repeat over and over. My first saying was a little chant he would yell with me, and he would say, "Who was daddy's baby girl?" and I would say, "Me, me, me!" I was very proud. . . . He always made sure we knew he loved us. He never didn't tell us. Something he always would say is, "I love you tons and tons and tons and tons." It was like a rhythm, and so we always said it to him. And so I know that I will never question from my father and I'm so lucky and so blessed to know that my Papa loves me. I love you, Daddy. Tons and tons and tons and tons.

He was a teacher. So, when I first got married, we brought our son out here, he was one. And this is a story my husband still shares fifteen years later. He was kind of giving us advice on marriage. It was mainly toward my husband. (Probably toward me too). It was about marriage and communication. He provided a story, which I won't share as well as he did, but I'm gonna share it with you. When he was married to my stepmom, Marisa's mom, they were driving, and he talked about how women and men communicate different. Women are a little less direct and they won't tell you, they'll kind of hint to you what they're saying when men will tell you straight to the point what they want.

Well, they were driving on the highway, and my stepmom said to him, "Bob Evans is at the next exit." And he's like, "Yeah, okay, whatever." He kept driving. So then he passes the exit and she said, "I'm hungry." And he goes, "Well, you didn't tell me." And she said, "I said Bob Evans is at the next exit." And so that story has stuck to my husband, and he shares that piece of knowledge. And not only does he share that advice. If we're not communicating well, and I'm not giving him exactly what I'm thinking, he says, "Is this a 'Bob Evans is at the next exit?'" . . .

I remember when I was younger, . . . he would say not many people would ask him about his day. . . . He said that many people would do that to him, and he always took in everybody else. And so, when he taught me that, whenever I got in a phone conversation with him or when I was in his presence, I was mindful to ask him, "How are you?" and really want to know and be present and understand what he was going through. Not just with his conversations but with others. I just want to share that knowledge, and for you to be mindful, and not to only be giving your "how you're doing," but to ask and to listen.

As I wrote this, I briefly shuffled through some of his journals that I didn't realize how much gold was in there. I just thought it was phone numbers and whatever. But as I wrote this, I know that being in the moment meant a lot to him. Just to know that you will never be in this moment again with these people. And to just really appreciate that. So again, I was shuffling through his journal and there were some notes about being in the moment, and these are the final things that I want you to think.

"How do you be in the moment? And what is that moment telling you? And what do you think the biggest need is for?"

Thank you all, and I just want to let you know: I'm his favorite.

Marisa Garverick-Herrera

Hello, I'm Marisa, I'm the baby of the family. And since I'm the last speaker, let the record show that I am the favorite. Welcome, or as my father would say, "Hola todx! Merry Christmas, felicidades. Happy birthday, happy New Year, happy Easter!"

My father is here, and he is content. In your presence, my father sees solidarity. In the warmth of the many embraces my family has received, my father feels comfort. And the tears on so many of your faces—my father is ready to ask what hurts, and to listen to your worries and together to find a path through struggle.

Because even in death, my father continues to organize as I can see, looking out at all of you here. Let us take a deep breath to inhale the profound power of community.

Rubén Castilla Herrera, *presente*.

In moments like this, our minds struggle to understand our hearts, and we are often left without words. My father recently told me that when he struggled for words, that was because there were none. Which is hilarious to me, and as Nick said, he never struggled for a word in his life.

Today, rather than words, his influence fills this room. His tireless pursuit of justice holds up the rafters; his memory occupies the space from wall to wall. Today, my father sits on that great activist perch, where there's nothing but song and dance. Because rebellions need soundtracks and revolutions need a little movement. My father now spends his days basking in the warm rays of his lifelong dreams, where every belly is full and everybody is warm.

And yet, while we celebrate his life, it is right to stare deeply into the void that he leaves. I can no longer laugh with him. I can no longer hear his stories. And I will not be able to dance with him at my wedding. His love will be there, but his person will not.

If you view the progression of life like Sandra Cisneros, she wrote, "The way you grow old is kind of like an onion, or like the rings inside of a tree trunk, or like my little wooden dolls that fit one inside of the other, each year inside the next one."

He also recognized, as she did, the healing power of crying, no matter one's age. Maybe one day, when you're all grown up, maybe you'll need to cry like you're three, and that's okay. Although I can no longer feel his abrazos, I can feel him in my tears, and I will hold him in my heart, siempre.

A week before he left us, my father wrote, "In times of joy, we believe we have been graced to be together. It follows that during periods of painful learning, this grace will not desert us." This is that moment of painful learning. Rubén Castilla Herrera, que en paz descansa. Rubén Castilla Herrera, *presente*. . . .

He said that whatever the struggle is, it is not to be taken lightly. That freedom, happiness, and love come from struggle. . . . So I ask you to do what you know to do, to do what brought you to my father. Lean into the struggle that he inhaled every single day.

Yesterday, I read a post by an organizer that perfectly articulated our mission in Rubén's absence. "You all just got promoted." So, qué vamos a hacer? My father had the answer. He said, "The leaders we need are already here."

Rubén Castilla Herrera: *PRESENTE.* Hasta la victoria siempre.

Afterword

by Nicholas Pasquarello

From the first stages of planning this book in honor of Rubén, I knew I wanted to contribute some of my own writing, but it was always hard to know where to start. Since chapter 5 already provides a close-up of the moments following Rubén's passing, it makes sense for me to pick up where that chapter left off and continue the story of what happened at the house.

As I mentioned in my interview with Paloma, when our neighbor Ashley drove me back from the hospital, our porch was pristine, cleaned up from the neglectful months of the winter season. This, among other spring cleaning activities, was what Rubén was working on that first beautiful day of spring. It was organized and mindfully decorated, as if he left one last gift for me before departing the physical world. I crumbled to the ground in tears.

Our home was something we cherished and were making our own over the past two years and four months we lived there. Our friends Patrick and Karen Kaufman owned the space and offered it to us to rent when we were looking to move. The moment Rubén and I entered the space, we looked at each other and both thought the same thing: "This is it. This is ours." In 2017, we moved in and, over time, began talking with Patrick and Karen about the possibility of buying the property from them.

In September of 2018, Patrick Kaufman tragically passed away from cancer. This personally started the hardest and darkest year of my life. A few months later, when Karen had the capacity to do so, we revisited our conversation about the property. This discussion had only moved forward slightly before Rubén passed some six months later.

Karen and I, now a widow and a widower, were going through the most difficult times of our lives. Karen lost the love of her life and father of her three beautiful children. Then she lost Rubén, a dear friend of hers and a close family friend who had been adored by her children.

For me, I first lost Patrick, a neighbor and close friend of mine. Then, months later, we lost Amber Evans, another close friend and a powerful community organizer, who had been admired and deeply loved by the social justice community, after a month-long period searching for her. As mentioned earlier in the book, Amber's death was officially ruled a suicide, which added its own unique layer of trauma. Then, the day after finally putting Amber to rest, I lost the love of my life, Rubén. Karen and I were in deep stages of grieving, but we processed this grief in very different, and, as it turned out, mutually beneficial ways.

After losing Patrick, Karen needed to purge herself of painful reminders of his absence. For Karen, her and Patrick's home became a traumatic space that amplified her grief as she was surrounded by objects and decor whose presence provoked painful memories of her loss. I grieved in the polar opposite way; our home was a space I knew I needed on a visceral level precisely because of the permanent reminders of Rubén.

While we lived together, the space had become a sanctuary for us on a level that felt sacred. After he passed, the sanctity of this space, and its preservation as something holy that could easily be despoiled, became paramount. I *needed* to be surrounded by and reminded of Rubén. I needed to feel his presence through the space he transformed and made our own. In addition to needing to leave her and Patrick's house, Karen needed to unburden herself of the other properties she and Patrick owned, including our home. Karen was relieved that I deeply wanted to retain the space and, eventually, after I finally graduated from law school in the midst of a global pandemic, we agreed on a purchase amount, and we transferred the property to my name in August of 2020.

After Rubén passed in April of 2019 until about November of 2021, I lived alone. The week immediately following his passing, the house was abuzz with many people from Rubén's family and community who visited, checked in on me, and wanted to feel Rubén's presence, which is unavoidable in the space.

After his service that was held the week following his passing, people trickled out, as they must. Family and community came together and collectively mourned, but eventually people needed to return to the realities of day-to-day life and their own responsibilities, families, and loved ones. The following week, my sister Chantal and my cuñado Chad stayed with me at the house. Once my sister got the news of Rubén's passing—which was, tragically, on her birthday—she booked a two-week stay for herself and Chad. They traveled all the way from Capetown, South Africa, where they live. She knew that the second week, the week after everyone started to file out, would be very difficult and I would need particular support then.

Of course, my sister was right. I definitely needed that support she and Chad provided that week. After they left, my friend Andrew Neutzling came to stay with me until I felt I was finally ready to be alone. At one point, Andrew proposed something he felt might help. He offered to move in. He wanted to keep an eye on me as I navigated the deep trenches of depression and apathy toward life. I didn't reject the offer entirely, but I basically told him, "You can do that, but you would be staying in the guest bedroom and you can't change anything about it. So that's up to you."

He understandably declined.

The house had two bedrooms, and Rubén and I would go back and forth as to where we slept. On April 5, 2019, we slept in the room we would use for houseguests, which we sometimes referred to as the "war room." The war room is plastered wall-to-wall with protest signs from over the years and other movement imagery. It reverberates with palpable movement and energy. I needed that room to stay the same. Exactly. The. Same. The painting on the walls needed to be the same, the posters needed to stay the same. My little Philadelphia Eagles flag and Rubén's (smaller) Dallas Cowboys flag needed to stay in the same position. So, if he were going to redecorate, Andrew's offer to move in with me was antithetical to the preservation of this sanctuary space.

When I finally felt ready, Andrew left, and I started living alone in our home and began the painful journey of trying to, one by one, pick up the shattered pieces of my life. While Rubén's presence was palpable, there was also an unbearable loneliness in the deepest trenches of the grieving process that my life had become.

Rubén's passing erected a number of permanent boundaries. First, I was to never love again. Second, love notwithstanding, I would never be in a relationship with anyone else, no matter how serious or casual. The mere idea of being in a relationship with anyone else felt foreign and offensive. Third, I would live in and preserve the house alone. Even if somehow I eventually opened myself up to being in a relationship with someone else, they would under no circumstances move in with Rubén and me. This was our space and ours alone. Eventually and—as I think whoever is reading this would hope—thankfully, these boundaries that once felt immovable began to shift. The shifting of these figurative boundaries manifested quite literally in the physical changes of our home.

I casually met someone named Edwin Woolever not long after Rubén passed. Gay men know what I mean by this. For the rest of you, I'll leave it up to your imagination. But suffice it to say this was a casual connection I had no intention of expanding. Edwin was also in a place in life where he felt very much the same. He was finishing his home, and by that, I mean he was completely restoring the house from the condition he initially purchased it, which was, to put it nicely, in shambles. He was getting ready to sell the house and relocate to Puerto Vallarta, Mexico, for an indefinite period, perhaps permanently. Neither of us had any interest in a relationship, and this was well understood between us.

When Edwin closed on his house and began making arrangements for his relocation, we started to spend more time together. This time was a bit more intentional than before. Looking back, we both knew we were feeling *something*, we just weren't sure what it was or what, if anything, to do with it. I gave myself permission to go on what I would describe as the first "date" I had since Rubén passed. I allowed myself to feel whatever I was feeling precisely because I knew it wasn't an option. I knew that whatever this thing was with Edwin was not going anywhere because he would soon be gone. Only under these conditions did I allow myself the grace of feeling this deeper connection.

When Edwin eventually moved to Mexico, we stayed in touch constantly through WhatsApp. We both knew there was something there, and I was okay with that because, again, it was not meant to go anywhere. I kept telling myself this. I clung to my boundaries.

Life did not go according to "plan" for Edwin or me, or the entire world for that matter. Edwin was at an impasse in Mexico. His work visa was denied and so he wasn't sure how long he could stay in Puerto Vallarta. One possibility he was exploring was to go to school back in Ohio to become a massage therapist. When the COVID-19 pandemic hit in March of 2020, this became a now-or-never moment for him, and he got on quite literally the last flight out of Puerto Vallarta before the airport shut down.

So now Edwin was back in Columbus. Fuck.

I was feeling many things that contradicted each other. On one hand, I was happy that Edwin was back. Whatever had started between us before he moved had grown since he left, and I wanted to see him. On the other hand, I was scared and disappointed in myself. I cursed myself for letting myself feel that deeper connection at the outset because this was at odds with the impenetrable boundaries I established. I had to reckon with what to do now that this connection I only allowed myself to experience because it was temporary was suddenly back again and staring me right in the face.

I am now a married man. Suffice it to say, those boundaries I set up like steel walls recoiled and shifted significantly. But this was, of course, a long process.

From the time Edwin came back to Ohio in April of 2020 to roughly November of 2021, he lived in a different home. First, he was in Olde Towne East, which actually was quite nice because it was a short walk from the old place on Franklin Avenue that Rubén and I shared for three and a half years. Then, he rented a place up in the Clintonville neighborhood. When I say "he" (Edwin) lived in a different space, what I really mean is *we* did. For all practical purposes, I lived with Edwin at these locations while essentially curating our home.

At first, our home was an inflexible space that I needed to preserve in precisely the way Rubén left it. Change nothing. I recall Edwin coming by one day while I was away at work to clean up the sidewalk outside the property. Fittingly, our home is the only house on the block without a cement sidewalk out front. Instead, it has beautiful, decorative brick. However, this beauty comes at the price of many more cracks in the ground where weeds can take root. Edwin came by to clean all of this up as a surprise one day while I was at work. I was immediately appreciative of this, until I found the pulled-up weeds in buckets in the back of the property. This was not okay. I did not tell Edwin it was okay for him to set foot on the property. I felt my boundaries were violated, and I let Edwin know how upset I was.

Looking back, I know I can't be faulted for feeling what I felt, but the situation was ironic and wreaked of privilege. I was totally okay to accept Edwin's generosity and labor. But how dare he step foot on my property?!

Thankfully, Edwin is understanding, forgiving, and unimaginably patient.

Bit by bit, my boundaries shifted and evolved. I was eventually okay with Edwin coming over. Only with me there, of course. And with what we now jokingly refer to as the ten-foot rule: no intimate contact permitted. We began doing work in the garden. As this was outside, it was a way to ease into the shifting boundary. When I say, "we began doing work in the garden," what I mean to say is Edwin began doing work in the garden. I don't, or didn't rather, know much about gardening. I lived surrounded by beautiful plants for many years, but they were all mindfully tended to by Rubén. I pull weeds and fetch things when tasked, but actually curating a garden? That was beyond me.

The first summer after Rubén passed, the garden was totally neglected. It was ugly and overgrown. It looked like how I felt. When I opened myself up to letting Edwin in the space, I started to realize just how dark that time had been. This next year, beautiful flowers will begin to bloom because they were tended to by Edwin. More importantly, Edwin was teaching me how to do this.

When I started learning this from Edwin, something incredible happened; I felt I was growing closer to Rubén. I was learning, enjoying, and appreciating something near to his heart that I didn't understand on this level before. And this was with the help of Edwin. I realized that being with Rubén and being with Edwin weren't somehow in conflict. Quite the opposite, I started realizing that not only could they peacefully coexist; my love for each could be reinforced by the other.

It still took a long time for me to finally feel comfortable with Edwin moving into our home. It took as long as it needed to take. During this time, the space was just being maintained, curated. In November of 2021, over one and a half years after Rubén passed and over six months after Edwin and I began our relationship, Edwin moved in. Those first few months after Edwin moved in, I realized how deeply I missed the space. I realized that by keeping this distance between Edwin and the home, I was creating distance between myself and the home. Given how important the space is to me, it dawned on me just how paradoxical this was. After Edwin moved in, I felt the joy of simply being home. As I began to regain my footing in our home alongside Edwin, I began to heal.

Like I mentioned earlier, Edwin is a professional restorer of homes. He's restored more than a handful of properties, quite literally tearing down and rebuilding the entire house bit by bit. Suffice it to say, he had a much better idea of what work needed to be done on the house than me, and there was a lot that needed to be done. Fittingly, the work began with the foundation. As with everything, a house is only as strong as the foundation upon which it's built. Edwin started doing what's called "tuck-pointing"—chipping away the mortar that binds the rocks that form the foundation of the home and then mending them back together. This is grueling, time-consuming, tedious work, something that, if done correctly, shouldn't have to be done again for several decades. Edwin was not just working on the surface with a short-term patch; he was making the foundation as strong as possible.

If the version of me in April of 2019 could see what the home looks like today, he would lose his shit. The day I write this, March 5, 2023, about half of the house is under construction. This half of the house includes the "war room." Remember? That's the room I swore not to take a single poster off the walls. Indeed, the space is changing dramatically. But I have trust in Edwin that the home will retain its character and magic.

While maintaining the character of the home, Edwin is quite literally building his own place in it. He is constructing what will be the main bedroom, which will have its own unique significance and character. In the process, I've learned that there's more than enough room in the home for both Rubén and Edwin.

No one will replace Rubén. No one could even come close. But this doesn't mean, as I felt it must, that I was left to walk the earth alone. And I know deep down, Rubén wouldn't want it that way. For a long time, "widower" was my primary identity, and I feared that if I strayed from that, this would somehow demean Rubén's memory or lessen the beauty of our time together. I've learned that, as with our home, there is more than enough room for Edwin and Rubén in my heart. And like the structure of the home, my heart grows stronger every day.

Notes

Introduction

1. Laura Engle, email interview with author, August 10, 2020.
2. Ibid.
3. Sarah Wynn and Ben Garbarek, "Columbus City Council passes resolution to keep immigrant families together," *ABC6*, February 24, 2019. Accessed October 26, 2022, https://abc6onyourside.com/news/local/columbus-city-council-set-to-vote-on-resolution-to-keep-immigrant-families-together.
4. Luis Noe-Bustamante, Lauren Mora, and Mark Hugo López, "About One-in-Four U.S. Hispanics Have Heard of Latinx, but Just 3% Use It," Pew Research Center, August 11, 2020. Accessed July 4, 2022. https://www.pewresearch.org/hispanic/2020/08/11/about-one-in-four-u-s-hispanics-have-heard-of-latinx-but-just-3-use-it/.

Chapter I

1. Jon D. May, "Tonkawa," *The Encyclopedia of Oklahoma History and Culture*, accessed January 31, 2021, https://www.okhistory.org/publications/enc/entry.php?entry=TO003.
2. Craig McClain, "How Presidential Elections Are Impacted by A 100 Million Year Old Coastline," *Deep Sea News*, June 27, 2012. Accessed November 27, 2021, https://www.deepseanews.com/2012/06/how-presidential-elections-are-impacted-by-a-100-million-year-old-coastline/.

3. Booker T. Washington, *Up from Slavery: An Autobiography by Booker T. Washington* (Dover Books, 2013), 160–161.
4. Roland Herrera, interview with author, July 26, 2020.
5. *Roadside America*, "Home of the World's Largest Pecan," accessed December 21, 2021, https://www.roadsideamerica.com/story/4031.
6. Matthew R. Martin, "The Two-Faced New South: The Plantation Tales of Thomas Nelson Page and Charles W. Chesnutt," *Southern Literary Journal* 30 (Spring, 1998), 17–36.
7. Rosaura Sánchez, *Chicano Discourse: Socio-Historic Perspectives* (Houston: Arte Público Press, 1983), 9.
8. Kelly Lytle Hernández, "The Crimes and Consequences of Illegal Immigration: A Cross-Border Examination of Operation Wetback, 1943 to 1954," *Western Historical Quarterly* 37 (Winter 2006): 421–44.
9. Rubén Castilla Herrera interview with Elena Foulis for *Oral Narratives of Latin@s in Ohio*, 2016, accessed October 23, 2022, https://cfs.osu.edu/archives/collections/ONLO/ruben-castilla-herrera.
10. Rosa María Herrera, interview with author, July 27, 2020.
11. Ibid.
12. Ibid.
13. Ibid.
14. Mitchell E. Shapiro, *Television Network Daytime and Late-Night Programming, 1959–1989* (Jefferson, NC: McFarland, 1990).
15. Roland Herrera, interview with author, July 26, 2020.
16. Ibid.
17. Ibid.
18. Ibid.
19. Donald Hodges, "Sandino's Mexican Awakening," *Canadian Journal of Latin American and Caribbean Studies / Revue canadienne des études latino-américaines et caraïbes* 19:37/38 (1994), 24.
20. Ibid, 25.
21. Ibid, 25–26.
22. Roland Herrera, 2020.
23. Jennifer R. Nájera, *The Borderlands of Race: Mexican Segregation in a South Texas Town* (Austin: University of Texas Press, 2015).
24. The siblings made no special note of the pecan.

25. Ed Hogan, "Sunny & the Sunglows Biography," *AllMusic*, accessed December 31, 2021, https://www.allmusic.com/artist/sunny-the-sunglows-mn0000588809/biography.
26. Roland Herrera, interview with author, July 26, 2020.
27. Broken Hearts. Facebook. Accessed December 31, 2021, https://www.facebook.com/543513389035229/photos/a.543516445701590/1647908261929064.
28. Guadalupe San Miguel Jr., *Tejano Proud Tex-Mex Music in the Twentieth Century* (College Station: Texas A&M University Press, 2002), 1–5.
29. Manuel Peña, "From Ranchero to Jaitōn: Ethnicity and Class in Texas-Mexican Music (Two Styles in the Form of a Pair)," *Ethnomusicology* 29:1 (1985), 29–55.
30. Ibid.
31. Roland Herrera, 2020.
32. Rubén Castilla Herrera, Facebook post, November 30, 2018.
33. Nicholas Pasquarello, interview with author, January 31, 2020.
34. Roland Herrera, interview with author, April 26, 2022.
35. Ibid.

Chapter II

1. Leticia Wiggins, "Rubén Castilla Herrera," *Dímelo Columbus*, February 15, 2017. Accessed October 26, 2022, https://u.osu.edu/dimelocolumbus/2017/02/15/ruben-castilla-herrera.
2. Cassie Bouska, Emily Dixon, and Bernadine Strik, "Growing Berries on the Oregon Coast: An Overview," *Oregon State University Extension Catalogue*, March 2018, accessed February 9, 2022, https://catalog.extension.oregonstate.edu/em9177.
3. Asher Elbein, "Cave's Clues Show It's More Than Just Oldest Outhouse in the Americas," *New York Times*, July 17, 2020, accessed February 14, 2022, https://www.nytimes.com/2020/07/17/science/cave-poop-americas.html.
4. David Lewis (Takelma, Chinook, Molalla, Santiam, Kalapuya), "Willamette Valley Treaties," *Oregon Encyclopedia*, accessed February 9, 2022, https://www.oregonencyclopedia.org/articles/willamette_valley_treaties/#.YgQei_XMKqB.
5. DeNeen L. Brown, "When Portland banned blacks: Oregon's shameful history as an 'all-white' state," *Washington Post*, June 7, 2017, accessed

February 18, 2022, https://www.washingtonpost.com/news/retropolis/wp/2017/06/07/when-portland-banned-blacks-oregons-shameful-history-as-an-all-white-state/.

6. "Railroad History of Portland, OR," Pacific Railroad Preservation Association, accessed February 9, 2022, http://www.sps700.org/gallery/essays/portlandrailroadhistory.shtml#:~:text=1871%20%2D%20The%20Oregon%20Central%20Railroad,that%20city%20on%20December%2023.
7. Roland Herrera, interview with author, July 26, 2020.
8. Richard Morris, Tamara Morris, and Tatiana Osipovich, "Old Believers," accessed February 9, 2022, https://sites.google.com/a/lclark.edu/rsco/immigrant-communities/old-believers.
9. Erlinda Gonzales-Berry and Marcela Mendoza, *Mexicanos in Oregon: Their Stories, Their Lives* (Corvallis: Oregon State University Press, 2010), 53–54.
10. Roland Herrera, interview with author, July 26, 2020.
11. Rosa María Herrera, interview with author, July 27, 2020.
12. Rubén Castilla Herrera, interview with Elena Foulis for *Oral Narratives of Latin@s in Ohio*, 2016, https://cfs.osu.edu/archives/collections/ONLO/ruben-castilla-herrera.
13. Rubén Castilla Herrera, Facebook post, February 14, 2019.
14. Roland Herrera, interview with author, July 26, 2020.
15. Rubén Castilla Herrera, interview with Josh Culbertson, *We Are Compatible*, podcast audio, October 10, 2017, https://wearecompatible.libsyn.com/rubn-castilla-herrera.
16. Renu Narchal, "Migrant children are often their parents' translators—and it can lead to ill health," *Psychlopaedia*, July 29, 2016. Accessed October 26, 2022, https://psychlopaedia.org/family-and-relationships/republished/migrant-children-are-often-their-parents-translators-and-it-can-lead-to-ill-health/.
17. I am told that their brother Guido, who had an artistic temperament, was often punished for not having the same earning potential as Herrera. He was once shut into their parents' closet for such a long period of time that when the adults finally freed him from his marathon time-out, they found him fully decked out in Nelly's attire.
18. Lynn Stephen in collaboration with PCUN staff and members, *The Story of PCUN and the Farmworker Movement in Oregon* (Eugene, OR: Center for Latino/a and Latin American Studies), 10.

19. Ibid., 12.
20. Rudolfo Anaya, Francisco A. Lomelí, Enrique R. Lamadrid, *Aztlán* (Albuquerque: University of New Mexico Press, 2017).
21. Foulis, 2016.
22. Ibid.
23. Jerry Garcia, "Latinos in Oregon" *The Oregon Encyclopedia*. Accessed February 11, 2022, https://www.oregonencyclopedia.org/articles/hispanics_in_oregon/#.YgZ-f_XMITU.
24. The Sunglows, "La Cacahuata," accessed February 12, 2022, https://www.youtube.com/watch?v=f6Xa5evczbw&ab_channel=verycoolsound.
25. Little Joe and the Latinaires, "Que tristeza me acompaña" (Virgencita de mi vida). Accessed February 12, 2022, https://www.youtube.com/watch?v=PvoOiU0Y0Bc&ab_channel=FLOREStejanoOLDIES.
26. Sarah A. Donovan and Jon O. Shimabukuro, "The Fair Labor Standards Act (FLSA) Child Labor Provisions," *Congressional Research Service*, June 29, 2016.
27. Neyza Guzman, JD, "The Children of YouTube: How an Entertainment Industry Goes Around Child Labor Laws" *Child and Family Law Journal* 8:1 (March 2020).
28. Statistics, The Center for Family Justice. Accessed July 16, 2022, https://centerforfamilyjustice.org/community-education/statistics/.
29. Luke Sprunger, "'This is where we want to stay': Tejanos and Latino Community Building in Washington County," *Oregon Historical Quarterly* 116:3, 278–309.
30. Ibid.
31. Roland Herrera, July 2020.
32. Roland Herrera, interview with author, August 3, 2020.
33. Thelma Sanchez Murphy, interview with author, August 27, 2020.
34. Foulis, 2016.
35. Sanchez Murphy, 2020.
36. Ibid.
37. "Methodist Church," *BBC Religions*, accessed April 7, 2022, https://www.bbc.co.uk/religion/religions/christianity/subdivisions/methodist_1.shtml.
38. "Methodism," *Brittanica*, accessed April 7, 2022, https://www.britannica.com/topic/Methodism.
39. Culbertson, 2017.

40. Foulis, 2016.
41. Nicholas Pasquarello, interview with author, May 28, 2022.
42. Ibid.
43. Roland Herrera, April 2022.
44. Ibid.
45. Ibid.
46. Eric A. Howald, *Keizer Times*, October 9, 2020. Accessed April 30, 2022, https://www.keizertimes.com/posts/2038/for-one-councilor-changes-to-city-charter-are-personal.
47. Jeffrey Markowitz, "AIDS Crisis Timeline," *History*, June 14, 2021. Accessed April 30, 2022, https://www.history.com/topics/1980s/hiv-aids-crisis-timeline.
48. Foulis, 2016.

Chapter III

1. Thelma Sanchez Murphy, interview with author, August 27, 2020.
2. "Bedrock Geology of Ohio," *Ohio History Connection*, accessed October 23, 2022, https://ohiohistorycentral.org/w/Bedrock_Geology_of_Ohio.
3. Jessie Walton, "The Forgotten History of Ohio's Indigenous Peoples" *Midstory*, July 16, 2020. Accessed October 23, 2022, https://www.midstory org/the-forgotten-history-of-ohios-indigenous-peoples/.
4. "Ohio Hispanic Americans: Snapshot from the 2019 American Community Survey," *Ohio Department of Development*, accessed October 23, 2022, https://devresearch.ohio.gov/files/research/P7002.pdf
5. Rev. I. F. King, DD, "Introduction of Methodism in Ohio," Ohio History Connection, accessed October 23, 2022, https://resources.ohiohistory.org/ohj/search/display.php?page=18&ipp=20&searchterm=Array&vol=10&pages=165-219.
6. Rubén Castilla Herrera, interview with Elena Foulis for *Oral Narratives of Latin@s in Ohio*, 2016. Accessed October 23, 2022, https://cfs.osu.edu/archives/collections/ONLO/ruben-castilla-herrera.
7. Naomi Chamberlain, interview with author, April 12, 2022.
8. Leticia Vásquez-Smith, interview with author, June 6, 2022.
9. Adam Slinger, "10 Years After 10 People Killed in Fire," *WSYX ABC 6* September 29, 2014. Accessed May 19, 2022, https://www.youtube

.com/watch?v=HBP6grEpqN4&list=PLfVejw4eD3ggQQkj1gkmQ5_1ZEdZ2O7Ke&index=19&ab_channel=WSYXABC6.
10. Foulis, 2016.
11. Deb Garverick, interview with author, April 2, 2022.
12. Naomi Chamberlain, interview with author, April 12, 2022.
13. Ruben Herrera Jr., interview with author, October 13, 2022.
14. Garverick, 2022.
15. https://my.americorps.gov/mp/listing/viewListing.do?fromSearch=true&id=104882.
16. Foulis, 2016.
17. Ibid.
18. Nick Torres, interview with author, June 20, 2022.
19. National Conference of State Legislatures, "Antiterrorism and Illegal Immigration Control Act of 2005," accessed June 7, 2022. https://www.ncsl.org/research/immigration/summary-of-the-sensenbrenner-immigration-bill.aspx.
20. Center for Immigration Studies, "Historical Overview of Immigration Policy," accessed June 6, 2022. https://cis.org/Historical-Overview-Immigration-Policy.
21. "Meeting Record," Latin@ Action Circle, October 27, 2009. Courtesy of Nick Torres.
22. Ibid.
23. Foulis, 2016.
24. Rommel H. Ojeda, "10 Years Later, Dreamers Say DACA Is Not Enough," *Documented* June 15, 2022. Accessed July 16, 2022, https://documentedny.com/2022/06/15/10-years-later-dreamers-say-daca-is-not-enough/.

Chapter IV

1. Peter Boag, "Sexuality, Gender, and Identity in Great Plains History and Myth," *Great Plains Quarterly* (1998) 18:4, 327–340.
2. Duane Brayboy, "Two Spirits, One Heart, Five Genders" *ICT* September 17, 2017. Accessed July 20, 2022, https://indiancountrytoday.com/archive/two-spirits-one-heart-five-genders.
3. Deborah A. Miranda, "Extermination of the Joyas: Gendercide in Spanish California," *GLQ* (2010) 16:1–2, 253–284.

4. Oscar Lopez, "Mexico sees deadliest year for LGBT+ people in five years," *Reuters*, May 15, 2020. Accessed August 2, 2022, https://www.reuters.com/article/us-mexico-lgbt-murders-trfn/mexico-sees-deadliest-year-for-lgbt-people-in-five-years-idUSKBN22R37Y.
5. Rubén Castilla Herrera, interview with Josh Culbertson, *We Are Compatible*, October 10, 2017. Accessed October 23, 2022, https://wearecompatible.libsyn.com/rubn-castilla-herrera.
6. Staff Writer, "Rainbow City: How Columbus Became So LGBT-Friendly," *Columbus Monthly* June 10, 2015. Accessed May 18, 2022, https://www.columbusmonthly.com/story/lifestyle/2015/06/10/rainbow-city-how-columbus-became/22788505007/.
7. Ibid.
8. Clare Roth, "Curious Cbus: Why Does Columbus Have So Many LGBTQ People?" *WOSU 89.7 NPR News*, August 28, 2018. Accessed May 19, 2022.
9. Ibid.
10. Culbertson, 2017.
11. Ibid.
12. This statistic varies widely, depending on the criteria used to define sexual experience. Alfred Kinsey's influential studies of 1948 and 1953 reported that 37 percent of males and 13 percent of females had at least some overt homosexual experience to orgasm, and suggested that a "continuum" more aptly describes human sexuality: a changeable quality in our lives with many gradients rather than a static assignment.
13. Culbertson, 2017.
14. Prince Shakur, "Ohio's Black Pride 4 Were Arrested at the Stonewall Columbus Pride Festival and Parade," *Teen Vogue*, December 6, 2017. Accessed June 4, 2022, https://www.teenvogue.com/story/ohios-black-pride-4-were-arrested-at-the-stonewall-columbus-pride-festival-and-parade.
15. Stephanie Watson, "Coming Out Later in Life," *Compass* by *Web MD*, March 30, 2021. Accessed August 6, 2022, https://www.webmd.com/healthy-aging/features/coming-out-later-in-life?src=rss_public.
16. Culbertson, 2017.
17. Ibid.
18. Marisa Garverick-Herrera, interview with author, August 31, 2022.
19. Leticia Vazquez-Smith, interview with author, June 6, 2022.

20. Rita Herrera, interview with author, July 12, 2022.
21. Rubén Castilla Herrera interview with Elena Foulis for *Oral Narratives of Latin@s in Ohio*, 2016. Accessed October 23, 2022, https://cfs.osu.edu/archives/collections/ONLO/ruben-castilla-herrera.
22. Todd Avery, "Students Strip Down in Protest," *UWire*, September 30, 2011. Accessed June 4, 2022, https://www.uwire.com/2011/09/30/students-strip-down-in-protest/.
23. Dorothy Hinchcliff, "Dallas Cowboys and Sweatshops," *Financial Advisor*, October 19, 2011. Accessed June 4, 2022, https://www.fa-mag.com/news/dallas-cowboys-and-sweatshops-8677.html.
24. Nicholas Pasquarello, interview with author, May 18, 2022.
25. Nelson Goodson, "Hernández-Serrano who tried to commit suicide multiple times was deported to Mexico on Tuesday," *Hispanic News Network*, January 31, 2012. Accessed June 4, 2022, http://hispanicnewsnetwork.blogspot.com/2012/01/
26. Vazquez-Smith, 2022.
27. Foulis, 2016.
28. Janice Fine, *Worker Centers: Organizing Communities at the Edge of the Dream* (Ithaca: Cornell University Press, 2006), 9–12.
29. Janice Fine, "Worker Centers: Entering a New Stage of Growth and Development," *New Labor Forum*, October 2011. Accessed August 11, 2022, https://newlaborforum.cuny.edu/2011/10/12/working-centers-entering-a-new-stage-of-growth-and-development/.
30. Janice Fine, "Worker centers: Organizing communities at the edge of the dream," *Economic Policy Institute*, December 13, 2005. Accessed August 11, 2022. https://www.epi.org/publication/bp159/.
31. Michael Smalz, email interview with author, September 6, 2022.
32. Steve Brown, "Columbus City Council Creates Wage Theft Commission," *WOSU* September 21, 2020. Accessed October 18, 2022, https://news.wosu.org/news/2020-09-21/columbus-city-council-creates-wage-theft-commission.

Chapter V

1. R. I. M. Dunbar, Clive Gamble, Gowlett (eds.) *Lucy to Language: The Benchmark Papers* (Oxford: Oxford University Press, 2014).
2. Thelma Sanchez Murphy, interview with author, August 27, 2020.

3. Jack Zimmerman and Virginia Coyle, *The Way of Council*, 2nd edition (Spring City, PA: Bramble Books, 2010), 28–36.
4. *Shambala: Making Enlightened Society Possible*, accessed September 5, 2022, https://shambhala.org/community/projects-activities/related-organizations/.
5. Awakin.org, "Speaker: Phil Cass: Transforming Leaders and Communities," accessed August 24, 2022, https://www.awakin.org/v2/calls/342/phil-cass/bio.
6. Rick Livingston, interview with author, August 24, 2022.
7. Parker Palmer, *A Hidden Wholeness: The Journey Toward an Undivided Life* (San Francisco: Jossey-Bass, 2004), 58–59.
8. Christina Baldwin and Ann Linnea, *The Circle Way* (San Francisco: Berrett-Koehler Publishers, 2010), 146–147.
9. Steve Ryman, interview with author, August 4, 2020.
10. Baldwin and Linnea, 148.
11. Erik Eckholm, "There May Be 'No Better Place,' but There Is a Better Slogan," *New York Times,* July 30, 2010. Accessed September 21, 2022, https://www.nytimes.com/2010/07/31/us/31columbus.html#:~:text=At%20least%20six%20earlier%20branding,expect%20to%20succeed%20by%20drawing.
12. "Art of Social Innovation," accessed September 21, 2022, http://aositoronto.weebly.com/four-fold-practice.html.
13. Coyle and Zimmerman, 5.
14. Ryman, 2020.
15. Paloma Martinez-Cruz, *Women and Knowledge in Mesoamerica: From East L.A. to Anahuac* (Tucson: University of Arizona Press, 2011), 75.
16. Marisa Garverick Herrera, Interview with author, August 31, 2022.
17. Rubén Castilla Herrera interview with Elena Foulis for *Oral Narratives of Latin@s in Ohio*, 2016. Accessed October 23, 2022, https://cfs.osu.edu/archives/collections/ONLO/ruben-castilla-herrera.
18. Becky Little, "Claiming 'Sanctuary' in a Medieval Church Could Save Your Life—But Lead to Exile," *History*, April 18, 2019. Accessed October 2, 2022, https://www.history.com/news/church-sanctuary-asylum-middle-ages#:~:text=The%20concept%20of%20sanctuary%20predates,part%20of%20Roman%20imperial%20law.
19. Dylan Yachyshen and Elizabeth Mather, "Rhetoric and the Trump Presidency: Hate Speech vs. The First Amendment," *Political Science*, March 2, 2020.

Accessed October 2, 2022, https://www.colorado.edu/polisci/2020/03/02/rhetoric-and-trump-presidency-hate-speech-vs-first-amendment.

20. Alice Speri, "After Going from Church to Church Seeking Help, A Mexican Family Finds Sanctuary in Philadelphia," *The Intercept*, December 25, 2017. Accessed March 8, 2023, https://theintercept.com/2017/12/25/after-going-from-church-to-church-seeking-help-a-mexican-family-finds-sanctuary-in-philadelphia/.
21. Nicholas Pasquarello, interview with author, October 2, 2022.
22. https://www.dispatch.com/story/news/local/clintonville/2017/09/11/sanctuary-for-local-immigrant-call/18835749007/.
23. Rev. Joel Miller, interview with author, October 11, 2022.
24. "Sanctuary for Edith," *Columbus Mennonite Church Blog*, accessed October 12, 2022, https://www.columbusmennonite.org/who-we-are/sanctuary-edith.
25. "Columbus passes ordinance protecting city's immigrants," *AP News*, June 6, 2017. Accessed October 12, 2022, https://apnews.com/article/3d68fa70f6a147939dae0fbbf640757e.
26. "Immigration Law: Sanctuary Cities," *Franklin County Law Library*, accessed October 27, 2022, https://fclawlib.libguides.com/immigrationlaw/sanctuary.
27. Steve Palm-Houser, *Columbus Free Press*, "Miriam Vargas Perseveres in Sanctuary without Her 'Angel,'" May 1, 2019. Accessed October 5, 2022, https://columbusfreepress.com/article/miriam-vargas-perseveres-sanctuary-without-her-%E2%80%98angel%E2%80%99.
28. Sarah Wynn and Ben Garbarek, "Columbus City Council Passes Resolution to Keep Immigrant Families Together," *ABC6*, February 24, 2019. Accessed October 27, 2022, https://abc6onyourside.com/news/local/columbus-city-council-set-to-vote-on-resolution-to-keep-immigrant-families-together.
29. Edith Espinal, interview with author, May 2022.
30. Edith Espinal, translation by author: "The importance of teaching us that we need to fight to come out of the shadows. Of not being afraid to struggle. Of not being afraid to fight. He was always willing to fight for others. He was always willing to help the community. I think that was what he taught us. You have to fight without fear if you want to move forward."

31. Patrick Cooley, "Activist's death ruled likely suicide," *Columbus Dispatch*, June 6, 2019. Accessed October 12, 2022, https://www.dispatch.com/story/news/crime/2019/06/06/activist-s-death-ruled-likely/4966937007/.
32. Nicholas Pasquarello, interview with author, October 2, 2022.
33. Steve Palm-Houser, "Miriam Vargas Perseveres in Sanctuary without Her 'Angel,'" *Columbus Free Press*, May 1, 2019. Accessed October 15, 2022, https://columbusfreepress.com/article/miriam-vargas-perseveres-sanctuary-without-her-%E2%80%98angel%E2%80%99.
34. Ibid.
35. "After 31 Months in Sanctuary, Columbus Mother Miriam Vargas is Free to Return Home to Her Family," *Faith in Public Life*, February 23, 2021. Accessed October 5, 2022, https://www.faithinpubliclife.org/news/after-31-months-in-sanctuary-columbus-mother-miriam-vargas-is-free-to-return-home-to-her-family/.
36. Documentary filmmakers Chris Temple and Zach Ingrasci created an eighteen-minute documentary titled *The Undocumented Lawyer* that was released by HBO in 2021. The film follows the remarkable life and work of undocumented attorney Lizbeth Mateo and profiles her involvement with Edith's journey in sanctuary.
37. Edith Espinal, translation by author: "I feel that there was more life that we could have shared. . . . Sometimes I feel like I didn't really take his presence into account. When I went downstairs at ten, at eleven in the morning, he was already there. I didn't realize that he was there to support me, that he was there for me. And when my son had an accident, he was the first to arrive to the hospital. He told them he was his uncle and visited him. Always. The two were always there. When Nick wasn't in school, he was there. It wasn't enough. There was much more to say. Much more to celebrate. This was going to be something that we celebrated together.
38. Naomi Chamberlain, interview with author, April 12, 2021.
39. Rev. Joel Miller, "Liturgy ~~1042~~ 1235," trans. Rubén Castilla Herrera with Andrea de Ávila and Christina Horst, *Voices Together* (Harrisonburg, VA: MennoMedia, 2020), 1042.
40. Rev. Joel Miller, interview with the author, October 11, 2022.

"Hasta la Victoria Siempre": A Trust the Circle Mix Tape

1. C/S or "Con Safos" is a Chicano expression used by some at the conclusion of a piece of writing, art, graffiti, or other forms of media that signifies "with respect." It also offers symbolic protection for its author, conveying a message along the lines of "this can't be messed with."

About the Author

Paloma Martinez-Cruz, professor of Latinx cultural studies at the Ohio State University, is the author of *Food Fight! Millennial Mestizaje Meets the Culinary Marketplace* (2019) and *Women and Knowledge in Mesoamerica: From East LA to Anahuac* (2011). She is the editor of *A Handbook for the Rebel Artist in a Post-Democratic Society* by Guillermo Gómez-Peña and Saúl García-López (Routledge). Her prose and poetry have appeared in *Nerter*, *Voces*, *PALABRA*, *About Place Journal*, and elsewhere. She produces Onda Latinx Ohio to showcase Latinx expressive culture in the Midwest.

Printed in the USA
CPSIA information can be obtained
at www.ICGtesting.com
JSHW062029120424
61091JS00010B/39